BATTLE OF BRITAIN DAY

BATTLE OF BRITAIN DAY

15 September 1940

Dr Alfred Price

Greenhill Books, London
Stackpole Books, Pennsylvania

Greenhill Books

This edition of *Battle of Britain Day*
first published 1999 by Greenhill Books, Lionel Leventhal Limited,
Park House, 1 Russell Gardens, London NW11 9NN
and
Stackpole Books, 5067 Ritter Road, Mechanicsburg, PA 17055, USA

British Library Cataloguing in Publication Data
Price, Dr Alfred, 1936–
Battle of Britain Day, 15 September 1940
1. Britain, Battle of, 1940
I. Title
940.5'421

ISBN 1-85367-375-7

Library of Congress Cataloging-in-Publication Data available

Publishing History
Battle of Britain Day was first published in 1990 (Sidgwick & Jackson, London)
and is now reproduced, complete and unabridged, exactly as the first edition.

Printed and bound in Great Britain by
Creative Print and Design (Wales), Ebbw Vale

Contents

Author's Note

In this account all times are corrected to British Summer Time. That was one hour behind Greenwich Mean time and the *Sommerzeit* in use in the Luftwaffe. In the case of people named in the text the ranks, positions and surnames (in the case of ladies who later married) were those held on 15 September 1940.

In the text German words have been anglicized. Thus Südel is written as Suedel, Gröger as Groeger and Plöhn as Ploehn. In the case of German unit designations, the closest English equivalent is given: Fighter Geschwader for Jagdgeschwader, Bomber Geschwader for Kampfgeschwader and Reconnaissance Gruppe for Aufklaerungsgruppe. Because they do not translate exactly, unit descriptions such as Staffel, Gruppe and Geschwader are retained. So are German rank titles (a list of equivalent ranks is given in Appendix A). Where the meaning is clear, the number has been omitted from German aircraft type designations; thus 'a Dornier' refers to a Dornier 17 and 'a Heinkel' refers to a Heinkel 111.

In several publications the abbreviations Bf 109 and Bf 110 are used for the Messerschmitt 109 and 110 respectively (Bf for Bayerische Flugzeugwerke – Bavarian Aircraft Factory). In official German documents written at the time, both the Bf and the Me abbreviations were used and both are correct. In this book the simpler abbreviation 'Me' is used.

It would have been impossible to write this book without the generous help freely given by so many people. In particular I should like to thank Arno Abendroth, Theodor Rehm and Horst Schultz in Germany for their help in reconstructing the Luftwaffe side of the story. In England Alan Cooper did a superb job searching through the official documents at the Public Record Officer at Kew; among other things, he assembled an almost complete set of the combat reports submitted by Royal Air Force fighter pilots that day. Herr Noack, curator at the Bundesarchiv Militaerarchiv at Freiburg, was extremely helpful in digging out records held there, as was Brigadier Lewendon at the Royal Artillery Museum at Woolwich. Those indefatigable researchers into the Battle, Andy Saunders and Peter Cornwell, kindly made available material they had collected during their own very detailed research and the latter made several valuable comments on the manuscript. Ron McGill passed me material he had collected. Others who assisted were Major John Ellingworth, John Vasco, Phil Goss, L. G. Smith, Michael Payne, Dilip Sarkar, Max Probst and Colin Brown. As always, Wing Commander Norman Hancock of the Battle of Britain Pilots' Association was extremely helpful. Wing Commander T. Neil kindly gave permission to quote from his superb autobiography *Gun Button to Fire*.

The Meteorological Office at Bracknell provided details of the weather during the 24-hour period. The National Railway Museum at York made available photographs of the damage to railway property. Many public libraries hold the wartime Civil Defence records for their area, and I am grateful for assistance from the staffs of the City of Westminster Archives, the Battersea District Library, the Central Library at Tower Hamlets, the Stratford Reference Library, the Borough of Southwark library, the Kent Archives Office, the Bromley Central Library and the City of London Guildhall Library.

Finally, and most important of all, I wish to record my grateful thanks to the participants who so kindly allowed me to record their stories. The research for this book was critically dependent on the information made available by those listed in the section which follows: 'The Witnesses'.

Alfred Price
Uppingham
Rutland
Leicestershire

THE WITNESSES

Witnesses interviewed by the author during the research for this book.

Ranks, unit locations, positions and names (in the case of ladies who later married) were those on 15 September 1940.

Police Constable Bill Albon, Staplehurst.
Squadron Leader Douglas Bader, Hurricane pilot, commander No. 242 Squadron, Duxford.
Pilot Officer Harry Baker, Spitfire pilot, No. 41 Squadron, Hornchurch.
Leutnant Hans Bertel, Messerschmitt 109 pilot, Fighter Geschwader 52, Coquelles.
Flight Lieutenant Minden Blake, Hurricane pilot, No. 238 Squadron, Middle Wallop.
Flight Lieutenant Peter Brothers, Hurricane pilot, No. 257 Squadron, Martlesham Heath.
Albert Brown, butcher, Battersea.
Charles Cain, trainee bank cashier, Beckenham.
Irene Cannon, civil defence worker, West Ham.
Violet Carter, housewife, Birkbeck.
Leutnant Roderich Cescotti, Heinkel 111 pilot, Bomber Geschwader 26, Wevelghem.
Walter Chesney, lorry driver, Streatham.
Sergeant David Cox, Spitfire pilot, No. 19 Squadron, Fowlmere.
Flying Officer Dennis David, Hurricane pilot, No. 87 Squadron, Exeter.
Wing Commander Lord Willoughby de Broke, senior fighter controller, No. 11 Group Headquarters, Uxbridge.
Dan Driscoll, delivery van assistant, West Ham.
Major Adolf Galland, Messerschmitt 109 pilot and commander of Fighter Geschwader 26, Audembert.
Reg Garman, Chief Engineer, Victoria coach station.
Unteroffizier Herbert Groeger, Dornier 17 radio operator, Bomber Geschwader 3, Antwerp.

Major Max Grueber, Heinkel 111 navigator, commander of IInd Gruppe Bomber Geschwader 53, Lille.

Pilot Officer Dick Haine, Blenheim pilot, No. 600 Squadron, Hornchurch.

Kathleen Hatton, embroidress, Vauxhall.

Feldwebel Rolf Heitsch, Dornier 17 pilot, Bomber Geschwader 76, Cormeilles-en-Vexin.

Jack Hill, air raid warden, Chelsea.

Hauptmann Otto Hintze, Messerschmitt 109 pilot, Erprobungsgruppe 210, Denain.

Sergeant Ray Holmes, Hurricane pilot, No. 504 Squadron, Hendon.

Sergeant Len Jeacock, Royal Engineers (Bomb Disposal).

Gwen Jenkins, shop assistant, Chatham.

Winifred Kingman, housewife, Battersea.

Feldwebel Heinz Kirsch, Dornier 17 gunner, Bomber Geschwader 3, Antwerp.

Oberleutnant Werner Kittmann, Dornier 17 navigator, Bomber Geschwader 2, Saint-Leger.

Oberleutnant Victor Kraft, Messerschmitt 109 pilot, Lehr Geschwader 2, Calais Marck.

Private George Lodge, Home Guard, Herne Bay.

Hauptmann Fritz Losigkeit, Messerschmitt 109 pilot, Fighter Geschwader 26, Audembert.

Sergeant Don Mackay, Headquarters, No. 307 Battery, Royal Artillery, Sittingbourne.

Ron McGill, schoolboy, Kennington.

Alexander McKee, waiting to join the Royal Air Force, Fareham.

Gunner Frank McMachan, No. 166 Battery, Royal Artillery, Chatham.

John Martin, private secretary to Mr Winston Churchill.

Tom Mercer, carpenter, Chatham.

Leutnant Herburt Michaelis, Dornier 17 pilot, Bomber Geschwader 2, Saint-Leger.

Albert Nicholls, vehicle mechanic, Chatham.

Oberfeldwebel Robert Olejnik, Messerschmitt 109 pilot, Fighter Geschwader 3, Samer.

Flight Lieutenant Bob Oxspring, Spitfire pilot, No. 66 Squadron, Gravesend.

Oberleutnant Dietrich Peltz, Junkers 88 pilot, Bomber Geschwader 77, Laon.

Oberleutnant Gerhard Ploehn, Dornier 17 pilot, Bomber Geschwader 2, Cambrai.

Flight Lieutenant George Powell-Sheddon, Hurricane pilot, No. 242 Squadron, Duxford.

The Witnesses

Feldwebel Wilhelm Raab, Dornier 17 pilot, Bomber Geschwader 76, Cormeilles-en-Vexin.

Feldwebel Theodor Rehm, Dornier 17 navigator, Bomber Geschwader 76, Beauvais.

Aircraftwoman Vera Saies, aircraft plotter, Headquarters No. 11 Group, Uxbridge.

Oberleutnant Peter Schierning, Heinkel 111 navigator, Bomber Geschwader 53, Lille.

Oberleutnant Hans Schmoller-Haldy, Messerschmitt 109 pilot, Fighter Geschwader 54, Campagne.

Feldwebel Horst Schultz, Dornier 17 pilot, Bomber Geschwader 3, Antwerp.

Frank Skinner, meat salesman, West Norwood.

Dorothy Slaughter, housewife, West Norwood.

Pilot Officer Paddy Stephenson, Hurricane pilot, No. 607 Squadron, Tangmere.

Unteroffizier Hermann Streibing, Messerschmitt 109 pilot, Lehr Geschwader 2, Calais-Marck.

Unteroffizier Heinrich Suedel, Heinkel 111 radio operator, Bomber Geschwader 55, Villacoublay.

Eric Sutton, schoolboy, Chatham.

Florence Tappenden, housewife, Chatham.

Freda Tomlin, farmer's daughter, Staplehurst.

Police Constable Bernard Tucker, Nine Elms police station.

George Tuke, schoolboy, Mayfield.

Lance Bombardier James White, No. 166 Battery, Royal Artillery, Chatham.

Oberleutnant Karl-Ernst Wilke, Dornier 17 navigator, Bomber Geschwader 76, Beauvais.

Flying Officer Alan Wright, Spitfire pilot, No. 92 Squadron, Biggin Hill.

Unteroffizier Horst Zander, Dornier 17 radio operator, Bomber Geschwader 3, Antwerp.

PROLOGUE

SIXTEEN THOUSAND FEET ABOVE the London borough of Brixton, 12.09 p.m. Throttle wide open and overtaking rapidly. Flight Lieutenant Peter Brothers of No. 257 Squadron swung his Hurricane into a firing position close behind one of the Dorniers at the rear of the German formation. Strung out behind in echelon to starboard, the other four pilots of his section followed. A 22-year old from Kent, Brothers already had eight aerial victories to his credit. Now he placed the glowing graticule of his sight over the bomber he had chosen as target, yanked the wings level and squeezed the firing button. Emitting a crackle like the tearing of calico, the fighter's guns spewed armour-piercing, incendiary and tracer rounds at a rate of 150 per second. Eight smoking fingers of bullets converged on the bomber.

Yet this action was not one-sided. Bright sparks of tracer streaked past the leading Hurricane as the German gunners enmeshed their assailant in a cross-fire. Brothers felt his plane take hits. 'The fire was coming not so much from the aircraft I was going for, but from the chaps to the right of him. But I didn't notice any immediate effect on handling so I continued with my attack.' After a short burst Brothers pulled sharply away from his victim, diving to clear the way for the second section of four Hurricanes to attack. Then the squadron split into ones and twos and the planes pulled round for further attacks on the bombers. More than a hundred British fighters were in the vicinity of the Dornier formation, buzzing round the bombers like angry wasps defending their nest.

The raiding formation comprised twenty-four Dorniers of Bomber Geschwader 76, one of them piloted by Feldwebel Wilhelm Raab. Raab, a 25-year-old from Dresden, had fought over Poland and France and was now on his 44th combat mission. He had flown fifteen times against England but had

1

never encountered such determined fighter opposition. Since passing over Ashford, about twenty minutes earlier, his unit had come under repeated attack. Now the enemy planes were charging through the formation with unprecedented ferocity. Raab concentrated on holding the plane straight and level for the final part of the bombing run, while behind him in the bomber's cramped cabin his gunners loosed off burst after burst at their tormentors. The Dorniers let go of their bombs, then, their task complete, the planes dropped their left wings and began a sweeping turn to take them clear of the target and the rumpus they had stirred up.

The fighter attacks continued without let-up. Shortly after leaving the target Raab felt his aircraft judder as it took an accurate burst. 'A glance at the revolution counters and . . . hell! . . . the left engine was running at idling speed. There was no smoke, no fire, but the propeller was going round so slowly that I could see the blades. Slowly we dropped back from the formation. We were about to become a very easy target for the enemy fighters.'

Raab's only hope was to dive for the billowing cumulus clouds far below. There he would be safe from attack. The German pilot pushed down the bomber's nose and its speed built up rapidly in the descent. But not rapidly enough. Several fighters detached themselves from the swarm and came bounding after the crippled Dornier. One of the Hurricane pilots, Flight Lieutenant George Powell-Sheddon of No. 242 Squadron, later commented 'We were on to him like a pack of dogs!'

Squadron Leader Brian Lane of No. 19 Squadron was pulling his Spitfire into position for another attack on the enemy formation when Raab's Dornier came past him.

> Reversing the turn I followed, firing from the quarter at the starboard engine. As I slipped in astern of the Hun, a Hurricane swam up beside me firing also. I turned to one side and saw two more Hurricanes behind him. Dammit! Who saw this Hun first?
>
> Then I realized that the Hurricanes had probably been chasing this Dornier when I had come in and attacked. Perhaps after all I was horning in on them! I looked back to see if there was anything else about. No – the sky was empty save the Hun, the Hurricanes, and me.
>
> Taking my place in the queue I waited my turn to fire. The German pilot seemed to be taking no evasive action at all, the Dornier was just diving towards the clouds. Getting impatient I

pulled out to one side and began a quarter attack aiming at the starboard engine again. This time I think I hit him, but it may have been one of the Hurricane pilots who was firing at the same time. The enemy aircraft began to dive more steeply.

For Wilhelm Raab that dash for cloud seemed to last for ever. 'There was a clatter like dried peas being poured into a bowl, announcing the arrival of more machine-gun rounds. Twice more our sick bomber was hit, before we plunged into the protective folds of cloud. Then we breathed a sigh of relief: we were safe from attack.'

Once in the billowing cocoon Raab learned that he and his crew had been granted no reprieve, merely a stay of execution. The plane's upper gunner had been killed during the final attack, and now lay slumped across his seat. The mechanisms controlling the pitch of both propellers had jammed. That meant that the pilot could not 'feather' the propeller on the 'dead' left engine, he could not turn the blades end-on to the airflow to reduce drag. Instead, the airflow was turning the propeller and with it the 'dead' engine, causing considerable drag. The right engine was undamaged, but because its propeller was jammed at the wrong setting it gave reduced thrust. Raab experimented with different flap settings, but to no avail; the remaining engine developed insufficient power to repeal the law of gravity. Even at the optimum flap setting the Dornier was descending at about a hundred feet per minute. At any moment the bomber would slide out of the bottom of the cloud. When it did, Raab and his crew would again face the enemy fighters but this time with virtually no defence against attack from the rear.

Suddenly the skies around the Dornier cleared and almost at once the bomber shuddered under the impact of bullets. The fighters were back!

By now Peter Brothers had joined the fighters hounding the German bomber. He took his Hurricane close behind the Dornier to finish it off, but his victim was flying much more slowly than expected. Brothers misjudged the rate of closure, and had to break off his attack abruptly to avoid a collision. 'I put on a lot of aileron to get the left wing down, to avoid hitting him. Then there was a bang: my aileron cable had snapped.' Rolling uncontrollably to the left, the Hurricane lurched past the bomber narrowly missing it.

Squeezed against his back-armour for maximum protection

3

from the enemy bullets, Wilhelm Raab watched the Hurricane sweep out in front. 'I glanced to the right and saw the enemy fighter come past me, banking steeply. Its wing missed mine by about half a metre.' Raab had no time to ponder on why his assailant had come so close, he had pressing problems of his own. The attack had severed the Dornier's aileron and elevator wires, and the plane had begun to slip from Raab's control. The German pilot ordered the two surviving crewmen to bail out, then he followed them out the cabin hatch.

Circling the Dornier with other British fighters, Brian Lane observed its final moments. Later he wrote:

> Throttling back, I dropped one wing to get a better view of the black-crossed aircraft. Behind, rushing over trees and hedges, fields and roads to meet the stricken machine, I saw its shadow. As the two came nearer and nearer a house loomed up, apparently in the path of the raider. With a sigh of relief, I watched it miss the obstacle. The shadow and master met with a huge gush of flame, as the aircraft hit the ground and the petrol tanks exploded.

The Dornier crashed near Underriver, just to the south of Sevenoaks.

Wilhelm Raab's parachute deposited him in a copse a few hundred yards from his blazing bomber. The silk canopy caught on the top of a high birch tree, leaving the German pilot swaying precariously in the wind. After several attempts Raab succeeded in grabbing the trunk of the tree. He locked his legs round it, then carefully reached down and released his parachute harness. 'I had never set foot on English soil before, and doing so now was no easy business. There were no footholds, the branches at the top of the tree would not bear my weight. And all the time the tree was swaying in the wind.' Slowly Raab edged his way down until finally he stood 'on English soil'. Shortly afterwards he surrendered himself to a civilian, who handed him over to a couple of Home Guardsmen.

Barely able to control his Hurricane, Peter Brothers eased the fighter into a rolling climb to gain altitude before bailing out. But as its speed fell away, the pilot found that his plane became progressively more responsive to the controls. At 150 m.p.h. and with the stick fully to the right, he found he could hold something approximating to straight-and-level flight. He looked out over the left wing and saw that the aileron was jammed fully up. No wonder the plane had rolled uncontrollably at high speed! Brothers edged the fighter up to 4,000 feet and carried out a brief handling check. 'I slowed to about 120 m.p.h. and discovered that I couldn't hold lateral control, she began to wallow. So I accelerated to 140 m.p.h. and found she handled all right.'

Brothers decided he had sufficient control to attempt a landing at the nearest airfield, and headed for Biggin Hill. He made a long flat approach and forced the protesting fighter on to the grass at 140 m.p.h., more than twice the normal landing speed of the Hurricane. Then, by skilful application of the brakes, he succeeded in bringing the fighter to a halt just short of the far boundary without standing the plane on its nose. Peter Brothers, too, was safely down 'on English soil'.

Both pilots had been lucky to survive the action on 15 September 1940. After the war Wilhelm Raab became a schoolmaster, teaching German children the English he had learned as a prisoner-of-war in Canada. Peter Brothers remained in the Royal Air Force and reached the rank of Air Commodore before he retired. During the research for this book the author interviewed both pilots and was able to bring them together for a second, much friendlier, meeting. It was a fitting sequel to a day neither man would forget.

PRELUDE

An Englishman's mind works best when it is almost too late.

Lord D'Abernon

SATURDAY 14 SEPTEMBER 1940. The Second World War had been in progress for just over a year. The four months since Winston Churchill had taken office as Prime Minister had seen an unremitting succession of military reverses for Great Britain and her Allies. Early in May German forces completed the occupation of Norway, and by the middle of the following month Holland, Belgium and most of France had fallen. Now the British Isles were threatened by the might of the Luftwaffe, and an armada of barges and small craft was assembling in ports along the north coast of Europe in readiness for the planned invasion.

The series of air actions now known as the Battle of Britain had begun in July, with dive-bomber attacks on convoys passing through the English Channel. The actions rapidly increased in ferocity, then, in the second week in August, the Luftwaffe shifted its attack to Fighter Command airfields. The intention was to secure air superiority as an essential prerequisite to the invasion.

As it had in previous campaigns, the Luftwaffe planned to overwhelm the opposing air force by bombing its airfields and by shooting down any fighters that rose to challenge the raiders. The attacks caused damage at several airfields in the south of England, but bomb craters could be filled in quickly and only rarely was a landing ground rendered unusable for more than a couple of hours. Fighter Command took a battering but it would never be defeated by such tactics.

Early in September the Germans sought another way to subdue their enemy: by a series of large-scale attacks on London itself. The new phase opened on the afternoon of Saturday, 7 September and caused considerable destruction to dock areas in the East End. More than four hundred civilians were killed and over a thousand injured. The shift to the new target took the defences by surprise and many RAF squadrons failed to intercept. In a series of scrappy actions that day Fighter Command lost twenty-eight aircraft, the raiding forces forty. That night, and on each of the nights to follow, German bombers returned to the capital bringing further death and destruction.

During the second daylight attack on the city, on Monday the 9th, cloud prevented accurate bombing. Twenty-seven German planes were destroyed for a loss of nineteen British fighters. Two days later, on the 11th, the Luftwaffe returned to the city, adding to the damage in dock areas. Fighter Command emerged from that action the loser – in shooting down twenty-three German planes, it lost twenty-nine Spitfires and Hurricanes. Three days later, on the 14th, German bombers attempted a further attack on the capital, only to be defeated yet again by cloud over the targets. On that day the losses were exactly equal: twelve planes destroyed on each side.

During each of the first four daylight attacks aimed at London, for one reason or another the British fighter controllers had failed to bring a major proportion of their force into action. In the case of the initial attack, the shift of the bombardment to the capital had come as a surprise and the fighters had been positioned to block yet another attack on the airfields. During the next three attacks, the cloud that hindered accurate bombing had also hindered the tracking of the German formations by ground observers, making it difficult to vector the fighter squadrons on to the raiders. As we shall observe later, this unconnected series of failures would lead Luftwaffe intelligence officers to make an entirely erroneous assessment of Fighter Command's ability to continue the battle.

THE REPORTS OF the bombing dominated the London newspapers for Sunday, 15 September, printed on the evening of the 14th. In an article in the *Sunday Times* Lord Elton wrote:

> It was bound to come. Who did not know it in his heart of hearts, even during those first deceptive months of 'phoney' war. Now that it has come, now that the first spiritual shock has been swiftly absorbed by the tough, resilient spirit of the people, it

behoves us to look coolly and closely both at and beyond the monstrous phenomenon. Is it an act of cold calculation or of reckless anger? That there is calculation in it is certain. As the Prime Minister warned us on Wednesday, the methodical preliminaries of invasion loom up along the whole length of coast from Norway to the Bay of Biscay.

But if the Germans felt that by bombing London they would shatter the determination of the British people to defend their island, Elton thought they were doomed to disappointment.

> The path which we have now to tread is steep and may be long, but it is not new to us. It is the path of Drake and the Armada, of Nelson and the flotilla of Boulogne . . . The old perils confront us, but even more menacing; the old stakes are to be played for but higher now than ever. It is the old enemy who assails us, but in another guise. London has made it clear that the old qualities are there to meet him.

The newspaper recorded that London's sirens had sounded six times during the daylight hours of the 14th. As was to be expected, the war had cast a long shadow over dealings on the stock market during the previous week:

> The Stock Exchange has given a commendable display of coolness under the conditions of last week. At frequent intervals business was interrupted by air-raid warnings, but this left ample time to execute the very moderate volume of public orders. These consisted largely of sales on behalf of deceased accounts or for urgent reasons connected with the war, and with public interest necessarily diverted into other channels investment demand was only on a moderate scale . . .

The columnist noted a fall in the price of rail shares, especially in those of the Southern Railway Company whose installations were now coming under systematic attack from the air.

Sport, too, was seriously affected and the newspaper's football correspondent wrote:

> Arsenal beat Fulham at Craven Cottage by a goal to nil, after a game that ended almost three hours after the kick-off. As though to emphasize the uncertainties of football these days, the final whistle had just gone when a second air-raid warning was sounded. They had been playing for eighteen minutes when the first warning came and they were called off the field. It was eighty-two minutes before the 'All clear' sounded and play was resumed.

9

Considering the magnitude of the perils facing almost every aspect of national life, the newspaper's racing correspondent took a particularly narrow view of the importance of his subject:

> Air raids have reached such an intensive form that the uninterrupted conclusion of any day's racing must be extremely doubtful, and time will show whether it will be practicable to carry out the list of fixtures already arranged. It is to be hoped that Hitler's Luftwaffe will not cause a complete cessation for the remainder of the war, for this would deal the bloodstock industry a blow from which it might never recover . . .

At the London Coliseum, *The White Horse Inn* was enjoying a long run, despite its Germanic setting. At the London Pavilion the film was *Dr Kildare's Strange Case* with Lew Ayres and Lionel Barrymore, while the Regal Cinema at Marble Arch was showing *The Westerner* with Gary Cooper.

IN ITS ISSUE for 15 September the *Voelkischer Beobachter*, official organ of the National Socialist German Workers Party, gave its view of the situation in the British capital:

London's First Week Without Sleep

> Relentlessly, the attacks on London continue. Since the beginning of the German reprisal attacks against the British capital, for the seventh time its population of 8 million were permitted no sleep. For 8½ hours during the night of Friday and Saturday, Londoners had to remain in their shelters. During the evening German bombers and fighters broke through the strong British flak barrage, and dropped accurate concentrations of bombs. These started new fires and caused further damage to installations of military importance. During the attacks damage was inflicted upon Buckingham Palace, the Palace of Westminster (seat of the higher and lower houses of Parliament), Downing Street and prominent business areas such as Regent Street and Bond Street which are the show places of the Empire. Bombs also fell in the vicinity of Piccadilly Circus and St Paul's Cathedral. The following morning Londoners barely had time to leave their shelters before, at 8.28 a.m., the sirens sounded yet again and they had to dash for cover.

Throughout, the German raids were described as 'revenge attacks' for those being carried out by the Royal Air Force on Germany. According to the German newspaper, London's idle rich continued to enjoy their accustomed life-style while the poorer inhabitants were left to their own devices:

In spite of considerable resentment from the sorely tried population, after dark there is a nightclub atmosphere in the basement shelters of the luxury hotels. Bands play dance music, champagne and whisky flow freely. Those parts of London not already deserted have become pick-up places for good-time girls and prostitutes offering themselves to the playboy plutocrats who have dodged conscription. Meanwhile, the abandoned women and children are left to find what shelter they can in a city largely gutted by fire.

Berliners saw nothing ironic in the fact that two of the city's largest theatres were performing plays by Shakespeare: at the State Theatre there was *As You Like It*, and at the Deutsche Theatre *A Midsummer Night's Dream*.

DURING THE afternoon of the 14th, Adolf Hitler presided over a conference at the Reichs Chancellery in Berlin, to discuss the future direction of the war. Senior commanders from all three fighting services were in attendance, with Generalfeldmarschall Milch deputizing for Reichsmarschall Hermann Goering who was on an inspection visit to units in France. After a review of the overall military situation the Fuehrer shifted the discussion to the planned invasion of England, Operation Sealion. Previous air attacks on Britain had been very effective, he said, and they would have caused even more destruction but for the hindrance caused by the weather. Undoubtedly the Royal Air Force had suffered heavily, but still the Luftwaffe had not achieved the degree of air superiority necessary if an invasion was to be launched. Grand Admiral Raeder, Commander in Chief of the Navy, agreed and went on to reiterate his view that an invasion should be undertaken only as a matter of last resort.

For the time being, Hitler continued, it was important to maintain the threat of invasion and combine this with further strong attacks on the British capital. General Hans Jeschonnek, Chief of Staff of the Luftwaffe, pointed out that attacks on military targets in the capital were unlikely to cause any large-scale breakdown in civilian morale, because most of the military targets and the docks were separate from the main residential areas. There followed a discussion on the wisdom of shifting the weight of the attack to centres of population, but Hitler was against this. It was the 'ultimate reprisal' that he wished to keep in reserve for the time being.

FOLLOWING THE Fuehrer's conference and a forecast of good weather over France, Holland, Belgium and the south of England for the next day, the 15th, staff officers at Air Fleet 2 headquarters in Brussels finalized plans for a double attack on London.

The target for the first attack, to be delivered at about noon, was the convergence of railway tracks in the borough of Battersea which formed a key section in the rail network around the capital. The tracks, running twelve abreast in places, linked the midlands and north with the south-east of England, and also carried traffic between the main-line stations at Victoria and Waterloo and their respective networks in the south of England. The conglomeration of lines included a couple of rail-over-rail viaducts vulnerable to bombing, making this a classic 'choke point' target sought by air attack planners.

The targets for the second, larger attack during the afternoon would again be the dock areas and warehouse complexes in the East End of London. The Victoria, Royal Albert and King George V Docks north of the Thames were to be hit, as were the Surrey Commercial Docks to the south of the river.

To Luftwaffe officers picking through the entrails of the available intelligence for evidence of Fighter Command's impending demise, the first four German daylight attacks on London seemed to provide a valuable pointer. In none of these actions had the bomber formations been engaged with the ferocity and effectiveness that had characterized many of the August actions. It looked as if Fighter Command might indeed be on the point of collapse, requiring a couple more large-scale actions to destroy its fighting effectiveness. If the German intelligence assessment was correct and Fighter Command really was at its last gasp, the correct strategy was to attack targets of such importance that the remaining British fighters would be forced to do battle – and thereby suffer further heavy losses from the escorting Messerschmitts.

If they were successful, the attacks planned for the 15th would advance the German cause in four important ways: they would knock out a focal point in the rail network, they would destroy large quantities of supplies imported from overseas, they would strike a blow against civilian morale by demonstrating London's vulnerability to attack, and lastly, and most of all, they would impose a further drain on the Royal Air Force's dwindling fighter strength.

ALTHOUGH THE LUFTWAFFE had suffered heavy losses in aircraft since the opening of the Battle of Britain just over a month earlier, most of these had been made good from reserves and new production. Compared with 2,226 serviceable aircraft on 17 August, on 7 September the three Air Fleets engaged in the battle possessed 1,895 – a reduction of about 15 per cent. During the Battle there had been a major re-grouping of Luftwaffe units. Air Fleet 5 in Norway had transferred its bomber and twin-engined fighter units to Air Fleets 2 and 3; and Air Fleet 3 in north-west France had passed most of its single-engined fighter units to Air Fleet 2 in north-east France, Holland and Belgium.

On 7 September, the date nearest to the 15th for which a full Luftwaffe order of battle was compiled, the three German Air Fleets possessed the following serviceable aircraft:

Air Fleet	2	3	5	TOTAL
Single engined fighters	533	90	35	658
Twin-engined fighters	107	22	–	129
Single-engined bombers	120	34	–	154
Twin-engined bombers	484	310	–	794
Four-engined bombers	–	4	–	4
Reconnaissance	51	58	14	123
Coastal aircraft	16	–	17	33
Total	**1,311**	**518**	**66**	**1,895**

(For a more detailed description of the Luftwaffe order of battle, see Appendix C.)

All of the units assigned to the daylight attacks on London on 15 September would come from Air Fleet 2.

DURING THE six weeks of intensive fighting, Royal Air Force Fighter Command had maintained its strength to an extent far greater than Luftwaffe intelligence officers had imagined. On the evening of 14 September the four fighter Groups possessed the following serviceable aircraft:

Group	10	11	12	13	Total
Spitfire	48	92	85	44	269
Hurricane	78	218	109	128	533
Defiant	–	18	14	7	39

Blenheim	11	35	16	14	76
Beaufighter	–	12	1	–	13
Gladiator	9	–	–	–	9
Whirlwind	–	–	–	4	4
TOTAL	**146**	**375**	**225**	**197**	**943**

(For a more detailed description of Fighter Command's order of battle, see Appendix D.)

Compared with the force available on 17 August, there were twenty-two fewer Spitfires and Hurricanes. But there were eight more Gladiators and Whirlwinds (the latter not yet operational),

RAF Group Boundaries.

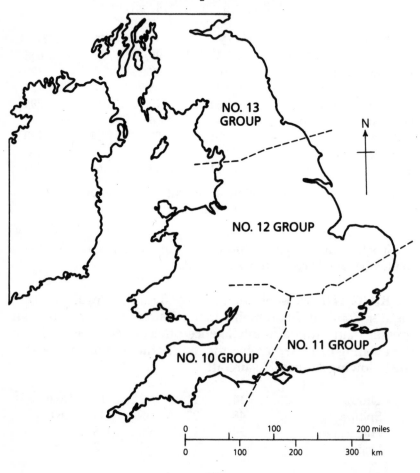

and the night fighter force had been increased by forty additional Defiants, Blenheims and Beaufighters. Thus the total number of fighters of all types was slightly greater than four weeks earlier.

Only a relatively small proportion of the British fighter squadrons was in position or properly equipped to engage escorted German bomber formations in the London area. The Commander in Chief of Fighter Command, Air Chief Marshal Sir Hugh Dowding, was responsible for the air defence of the whole of the country and not just the area around the capital. No. 13 Group in the north was too far away to take part in actions around London. So were most of the squadrons assigned to Nos 10 and 12 Groups. The squadrons equipped with Defiants, Gladiators, Blenheims and Beaufighters were unsuitable for operations where they might encounter German single-engined fighters. Thus, to meet attacks by escorted bombers against London, the Command could bring to bear only about three hundred Spitfires and Hurricanes – about a third of its total numerical strength.

During the Battle so far, Fighter Command had suffered a serious loss of experienced pilots. In the middle of September the Command had 1,492 operational pilots against an establishment of 1,662 – a deficiency of about 10 per cent. Many of the replacement pilots had come straight from the training schools and were ineffective unless led into action by experienced men. Previously it had been Air Chief Marshal Dowding's policy to move in fresh squadrons from quieter areas to replace those in the south-east as they became exhausted, while the latter moved north to rest and re-form. But by the beginning of September the casualty rate was such that the policy of rotating squadrons was breaking down; fresh squadrons committed to the battle became depleted before re-formed units were ready to take their place. Desperate times called for desperate solutions, and on 8 September Dowding reluctantly decided to split his squadrons into three categories:

> Category A units: Squadrons in No. 11 Group, and those in the Middle Wallop and Duxford sectors on its immediate flanks, which were to bear the brunt of the fighting. These units were to be kept at full strength both in aircraft and in pilots. Only if they suffered exceptionally heavy losses would these units be moved out of the battle area.

RAF Fighter Bases in South-East England, Group and Sector Boundaries.

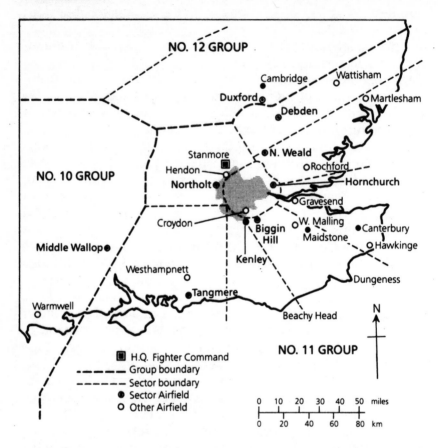

Category B units: A few outside squadrons, initially five and most of those in No. 10 Group, to be maintained at operational strength ready to be used as relief units if this became absolutely necessary.

Category C units: The remaining day fighter squadrons in the Command, which were to be stripped of operational pilots for the benefit of the A Category units, down to a minimum of five or six. These units were to devote their main energies to the training of new pilots. Although these squadrons would not be fit to do battle with enemy fighters, they would be capable of defending the quieter sectors against attacks by unescorted bombers.

Had it been continued for any length of time, the new policy would have had grave implications for the fighting strength of Dowding's Command, with the Category C squadrons becoming progressively less effective. But by the evening of 14 September the system had not been running long enough to cause a serious deterioration in the latter. The Category C squadrons were still capable of giving a good account of themselves, if they were thrown into the main battle.

GEOGRAPHY DICTATED that most of the fighting during this phase of the Battle took place between aircraft of No. 11 Group of Fighter Command and Air Fleet 2 of the Luftwaffe.

The commander of No. 11 Group was Air Vice-Marshal Keith Park, a 48-year-old New Zealander who had flown fighters over France during the First World War and ended the conflict with twenty victories to his credit. Over six feet tall, gaunt and austere-looking, Park was a devout Christian who drew great strength from his religion. Now his air defence fiefdom comprised the whole of the south-eastern corner of England, to a line running approximately from Southampton, via Aylesbury, to Lowestoft. While major air actions were in progress over the area Park's place was at his underground operations room at Uxbridge, where the staff worked feverishly to collate and set out in readily usable form the mass of reports flowing in from the web of radar stations and Observer Corps posts throughout the country. As we shall see, this was the information on which Park based his decisions. Between actions, flying his personal Hurricane, Park paid frequent visits to his squadrons to gain a first-hand impression of the progress of the Battle. An energetic and popular leader, Park had the rare gift of being able to make those around him feel that their views mattered.

The commander of Air Fleet 2, Generalfeldmarschall Albert Kesselring, had served in the army during the First World War and risen to the post of brigade adjutant. An extremely capable administrator, he had transferred to the new Luftwaffe when it formed in 1933 and became head of that service's Administrative Office. Kesselring was promoted to general in 1934 and held a succession of progressively more important posts. In 1938 he was appointed commander of Air Fleet 1 and led that formation during the campaign in Poland. Early in 1940 he moved to take command of Air Fleet 2, the largest such formation in the west, in preparation for the planned offensive against France, Belgium and Holland. Now, with its headquarters at Brussels, his Air Fleet was the strongest of those deployed against England and it controlled all Luftwaffe units based in Holland, Belgium and France as far west as the Seine. Kesselring was a German officer of the old school; with a ready smile, he was firm but always courteous with subordinates, and greatly respected. Like Park he had the gift of being able to inspire others, and, had the circumstances been different, it is likely that the two men would have found that they had much in common.

THUS THE two sides faced each other on 14 September 1940. In the chapters that follow we shall see how each made use of its forces on the following day.

Chapter 1

INITIAL SKIRMISHES

Midnight to 10.10 a.m.

When war begins, the Devil makes Hell bigger.

John Ray

AS MIDNIGHT chimed and 15 September began its eventful course, London was in the middle of its eighth consecutive night of aerial bombardment. From high above the city came the waam-waam note of bombers' engines punctuated by the distant 'crump' of detonating anti-aircraft shells. Searchlight beams probed the sky, like surgical scalpels delving into some vast open wound. Above the city the skies were clear, and the bright harvest moon bathed its blacked-out buildings in a silky sheen. On the ground the otherwise idyllic scene was shattered at irregular intervals by the drum-roll of bombs exploding in rows, the staccato bark of the anti-aircraft guns and the clanking bells of fire engines and rescue vehicles racing to their urgent assignations.

Shortly after midnight there was a short respite, as the last of Air Fleet 3's bombers completed their attacks and headed for their bases in north-west France (for details of the raiding forces, see Appendix E). The attack resumed at 0.50 a.m. with the arrival of the first bombers from Air Fleet 2. Eleven Heinkels of Bomber Gruppe 126 delivered their bombs, but then the weather took a hand in the proceedings. Patches of strato-cumulus cloud started drifting over the capital from the north-west and during the next hour the overcast became complete. It was godsend for the citizens of London, protecting them far more effectively than their man-made defences.

Bomber Geschwader 4 was to have dispatched forty-six

19

Heinkels to attack the city, but rain and low cloud over its bases in Holland led to the plan being abandoned after only five of the bombers had taken off. The first of these arrived over London at 2 a.m. and their diffuse attack lasted three-quarters of an hour.

That night the main concentrations of bombs fell in the Chelsea, Fulham and Westminster areas. In these boroughs there was damage to residential property, with nineteen people killed and thirty-one injured. The worst single incident was when a bomb hit the Church of the Holy Redeemer in Chelsea, where several people had been sheltering in the vaults; fourteen were killed and twenty-six injured. Elsewhere in the capital, a bomb damaged the roof of Cannon Street station and the building had to be closed until the structure was made safe. In a separate incident, traffic through Clapham Junction station was halted after an unexploded bomb was found embedded in the track beside one of the platforms.

Small raiding forces were also active over other parts of the country. Bombs fell in the Cardiff, Bootle, Leicester and Ipswich areas. The only significant damage was at Bootle, where a railway shed and sidings at the West Alexandra Dock were hit.

Shortly after midnight a Heinkel 115 floatplane on armed reconnaissance off Montrose located the freighter *Nailsea River* (5,548 tons) in the moonlight and sank it with a torpedo. Soon afterwards the freighter *Halland* was also sunk by air attack in the same area.

From 3.30 a.m., eleven Heinkel 115 floatplanes of Bomber Gruppe 106 flew singly up the Thames Estuary to plant magnetic mines in the shipping lanes. Elsewhere, mines were dropped in the Bristol Channel, Liverpool Bay and Milford Haven, and off Hartlepool, Berwick and Aberdeen.

That night Fighter Command flew twenty-eight sorties. Most were by Blenheims, though a few Beaufighters, Spitfires and Hurricanes also took part. Later the Royal Air Force would develop its night interception techniques to a fine art, but in the summer of 1940 they were in their infancy. The night fighters patrolled outside the gun-defended areas, on lines astride the bombers' approach routes, and tried to catch the enemy planes as they came past. Few of the night fighters carried radar, and in any case the early sets were short-ranging and unreliable. Those crews lacking the device had only their eyes with which to locate the raiders.

Searchlights were of limited value in locating the enemy bombers. Pilot Officer Dick Haine of No. 600 Squadron, one of those on patrol in a Blenheim during the early morning darkness of the 15th, explained:

> It might seem a simple matter for night fighter crews to see bombers that had been illuminated by searchlights, but this was not the case. If the raiders came on bright moonlight nights [as was the case on 15 September], the beams of the searchlights were not visible at heights much above 10,000 feet.
> If the searchlights were actually on the enemy bomber the latter could be seen from some way away, but only if the fighter was beneath the bomber and could see its illuminated underside. If the fighter was higher than the bomber, the latter remained invisible to the fighter pilot. If there was any haze or cloud [there were both during the early hours of the 15th] it tended to diffuse the beams so there was no clear interesection to be seen, even if two or more searchlights were following the target.

Moreover, if a raider was seen from below, the Blenheim's margin of performance over the German bombers was so small that usually the fighter could not reach an attacking position. During the night of 14/15 September no RAF night fighter crew reported having engaged an enemy aircraft. However, a Heinkel of Bomber Geschwader 4 returned with minor damage and its crew reported having been attacked by a fighter. Almost certainly the airmen were mistaken and the damage had been caused by ground fire.

The anti-aircraft gun defences of London, Cardiff and Liverpool went into action, but made no claims.

ROYAL AIR FORCE bombers were also active during the night of the 14th/15th, with a total of 157 sorties by Battles, Blenheims, Hampdens, Whitleys and Wellingtons. Ninety-two of the sorties were against the ports where the German invasion fleet was assembling: Boulogne, Calais, Ostend, Dunkirk and Antwerp. The remaining bombers penetrated deeper into enemy territory, going for a range of targets including the marshalling yards at Brussels, Hamm and Krefeld. One bomber, a Whitley, failed to return from the night's operations and German records indicate that it was shot down by flak over Holland.

The Weather Situation, 07 hours GMT (8 a.m. British Summer Time) on 15 September 1940.

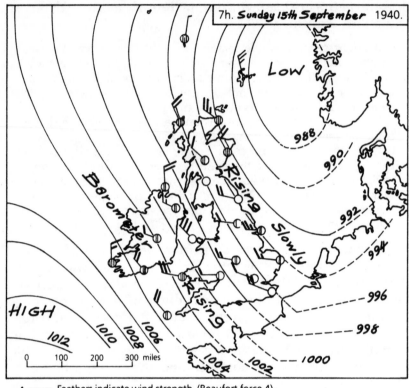

7h. **Sunday 15th September** 1940.

Feathers indicate wind strength (Beaufort force 4)
Wind direction (NW)
Circle indicates position of weather station
Two bars across circle indicates half cloud cover.

FIRST LIGHT on 15 September was at 6.34 a.m., and during the next three-quarters of an hour the sun's disc rose above the eastern horizon. That day the weather over Britain was dominated by a deep depression off the south-east of Norway, and an associated area of high pressure over the Azores. Pressure was slowly rising, giving an unsettled weather picture. Off the Orkneys the north-westerly wind was rising to gale force. By dawn the layer of strato-cumulus over London had dispersed, leaving only a few puffs at 1,000 to 2,000 feet and a trace of stratus higher up. At ground level the visibility was four miles, limited by a light mist. The temperature was a mild 14 degrees Centigrade (57 degrees F).

ON THIS THIRD Sunday in September many planned to go to church to pray for Britain's deliverance in the difficult times ahead. Yet at St Paul's Cathedral, the nation's most famous place of worship, all services had been cancelled. During the small hours of the previous Thursday, the 12th, a 2,200-pound bomb had smashed through the pavement at Dean's Yard immediately beside the South West Tower, entered the wet subsoil and sunk twenty-seven feet below ground level. Fortunately the bomb – the largest in general use in the Luftwaffe – failed to explode. Police cordoned off the area, and a team of Royal Engineers under Lieutenant Robert Davies began the potentially dangerous task of extricating the bomb.

By the morning of the 15th work was well advanced on the vertical timbered shaft leading to the bomb. In its passage through the ground the bomb had smashed through a gas main and the escaping gas had ignited. Even after the gas had been turned off and the fire extinguished, soldiers digging towards the bomb encountered pockets of gas and some had to be helped to the surface after inhaling it.

Sergeant Len Jeacock, a member of another bomb disposal team, visited the St Paul's site while the work was in progress. 'When I got to the site they had not reached the bomb, though they were well on their way to it. By then it was a completely straightforward operation,' he recalled. 'Above the shaft a set of sheerlegs had been set up, that supported a pulley from which a bucket was lowered into the shaft to pick up the spoil. At any time there would be three men working in the shaft, two at the bottom digging and a third at the top pulling up the bucket and passing down pieces of timber to shore up the sides of the 8-foot by 6-foot shaft. The work went on in shifts around the clock.'

The term 'completely straightforward' was, of course, relative only to what was normal to a bomb disposal operation. Even discounting the risk of an explosion, there remained the not-inconsiderable matter of digging out by hand more than seventy tons of subsoil. Because the bomb threatened a major item of the nation's heritage, the sappers had orders to continue work even when air-raid warnings were in force. Sirens in that part of London had sounded eleven times since the discovery of the bomb, and work had continued throughout.

OVER SOUTHERN England the day began quietly enough, and the first excitement for Fighter Command's day fighter squadrons did not come until shortly after 8 a.m. Then the coastal radar stations picked up an unidentified aircraft heading westwards up the Channel. The British radar operators suspected that it was a reconnaissance aircraft on a routine mission, and they were right: it was a Heinkel 111 of Weather Reconnaissance Staffel 51, based at Orly near Paris.

The filter room at Fighter Command Headquarters designated the intruder 'Raid 16', and tracked it approaching the Devonshire coast. At 8.30 a.m. the intruder came within interception range of fighters based at Exeter, and No. 87 Squadron received orders to scramble a pair of Hurricanes.

For Flying Officer Dennis David and Pilot Officer Trevor Jay, the scramble order brought an abrupt end to their fitful night's sleep on camp beds in the squadron's readiness hut. The two pilots pulled uniform jackets and trousers over their pyjamas, slid on socks and flying boots and donned their yellow life jackets. Still sleepy, they trotted to their fighters parked nearby and struggled into the cockpits. While a mechanic helped each man strap in, the planes' Merlin engines burst into life belching clouds of grey smoke. The Hurricanes edged out of their dispersals, then the noise rose to a crescendo as they accelerated across the grass in a series of bounds that grew progressively longer. The fighters lifted off the ground and their stalky undercarriage legs swung upwards and inwards into their housings. With David in the lead, the Hurricanes curved on to a south-westerly heading. As the sound of fast-revving engines receded into the distance, the morning stillness returned to Exeter.

Under the direction of Flight Lieutenant Dudley Mumford, senior fighter controller at Exeter, the fighters climbed to 6,000 feet and headed out to sea. A few minutes later David caught sight of the enemy plane. The Heinkel was between him and the coast – the fighters had cut off its retreat. 'It was a funny sort of day, with layers of cloud both above and below the Heinkel. It seemed the pilot was experienced, when he saw us he turned south trying to get away,' David later recalled. 'He was trying to get back into cloud. But we had plenty of speed, we were on to him before he got there.'

Closing fast, David swung behind the intruder and delivered two four-second bursts from short range. 'I was never any good at long distance firing so I would always get in very close,' he told the author. David saw his rounds striking the enemy aircraft, then he had to bank steeply to avoid colliding with the bomber. Next, Jay ran in to attack the Heinkel from behind and fired a long burst from 200 yards and another from 50 yards.

The German aircraft was in serious trouble. 'I could see petrol streaming from both wings, like a plume. The port engine had stopped and the undercarriage dropped down – that always seemed to happen when a Heinkel's hydraulic system was damaged. The aircraft went into a steep diving turn into cloud and disappeared from our view,' David remembered. Although they did not see it crash, both British pilots were convinced that the enemy aircraft would not get home.

From German documents it is clear that an SOS was received from the crippled aircraft before it crashed into the sea. A Heinkel 59 rescue floatplane was scrambled from Cherbourg to search the area, but it would return three hours later having found nothing of the plane or its crew of five. The air fighting on 15 September had claimed its first victims.

THROUGHOUT THE rest of the morning other German reconnaissance aircraft were tracked on radar making their individual ways to targets in Great Britain. A Junkers 88 photographed the airfields at Pembrey, Sealand and Woodford, and the cities of Manchester, Liverpool and Birkenhead. Another of these aircraft photographed the airfields at Netheravon, Benson and Eastchurch, the oil refinery at Thames Haven and the Royal Navy base at Chatham. Yet others were tracked coming in over Spurn Head, Lowestoft, Harwich, Dungeness and the Isle of Wight. Sections of fighters were sent after the high-flying intruders, but photographic reconnaissance planes were difficult targets and none would be shot down on this day.

THE RELATIVE quiet over southern England would not last much longer. Shortly after 10 a.m., at airfields near Paris, elements of two Gruppen of Dornier 17s were preparing to take off. For the first major attack of the day the target was in the centre of London, a move calculated to stir Royal Air Force Fighter Command into action. In that aim the German planners would succeed beyond their wildest expectations.

Chapter 2

THE NOON ATTACK ON LONDON

10.10 a.m. to 1.00 p.m.

Surprise is obtained by opposing the enemy with a great many more troops than he expected at some particular point. The superiority in numbers in this case is very different to an overall superiority in numbers; it is the most powerful instrument in the art of war.

Von Clausewitz

CORMEILLES-EN-VEXIN AIRFIELD NEAR PARIS, 10.10 A.M. Engines ticking over, nineteen Dornier 17s of the IIIrd Gruppe of Bomber Geschwader 76 sat three-by-three in squat rows at one end of the grass landing ground. A green flare soared into the sky in front of the planes: the signal to take off. In each of the three bombers at the head of the line, the pilot thrust forward the throttles with his left hand. The engine roar rose to a crescendo and the planes surged forward, wings rocking as they gathered speed over the uneven surface. Almost in unison the Dorniers lifted off the ground and climbed away slowly, like vultures with over-full bellies leaving a carcass. Behind them, the next three bombers commenced their take-off runs. The rest of the planes followed in turn.

Major Alois Lindmayr, 38, commanding the IIIrd Gruppe, flew as navigator in the leading Dornier. An experienced officer, he had been awarded the Ritterkreuz for leading daring low-level attacks against airfields and other targets during the Battle of France. Many of the unit's crews were seasoned veterans, though there was also a leavening of inexperienced men recently arrived to replace losses.

The leading bombers flew straight ahead until they reached 1,500 feet. Then they levelled off, turned through a semi-circle and headed back to the airfield. On the way, the Dorniers that had taken off after them curved into their assigned positions behind. Once assembled, the formation turned north and was soon out of sound and sight of those watching on the ground.

At Beauvais, twenty miles north of Cormeilles, a similar scene was enacted as eight Dorniers of the Geschwader's Ist Gruppe also took off and formed up. Normally a bomber Gruppe had enough serviceable planes to put up a 27-plane formation by itself. But these were not normal times. After six weeks of hard fighting over England, Bomber Geschwader 76 was well below establishment in both planes and crews. Now two of its Gruppen had to be employed to do the work of one. Moreover, many of its Dorniers were in poor shape; the one Feldwebel Wilhelm Raab was flying had emerged from the workshop only that morning, patched up after being damaged in a previous action.

Near Amiens the two groups of Dorniers joined formation, began their climb to attack altitude and headed for Cap Gris Nez to rendezvous with their escorting Messerschmitts.

The attacks on England had drawn a venomous response from the defending fighters, and German bomber units had been forced to explore every possible avenue to protect themselves. As an experiment, Feldwebel Rolf Heitsch's Dornier had an infantry flame-thrower fitted in the fuselage pointing rearwards. Today the 'secret weapon' was to be tested in action for the first time. Even if the jet of flame failed to set enemy fighters ablaze, it might deter them from closing to short range to attack. If it proved effective the weapon was to be fitted to other bombers.

NO. 11 GROUP HEADQUARTERS, UXBRIDGE, 10.30 A.M.
The take-off and form-up by Bomber Geschwader 76 had taken place well beyond the view of early warning radar stations along the south coast of England. At the Uxbridge headquarters of No. 11 Group of Fighter Command there was excitement that morning, but of a different sort. Air Vice-Marshal Keith Park had just received word that the Prime Minister, Winston Churchill, was on his way from Chequers to pay a snap visit.

John Martin, private secretary with the Prime Minister that day, told the author: 'Mr Churchill would often do a thing like that on the spur of the moment. He liked to drive very fast and would urge the driver to go faster. The car was fitted with a police gong so it could ignore traffic lights and hazards like that; there was very little traffic anyway.'

Carrying the Prime Minister, Mrs Churchill, Martin, an armed bodyguard and a driver, the car rapidly covered the sixteen miles to the headquarters. With staff officers in attendance, Park waited at the entrance of his command bunker to receive the important visitors. When the Prime Minister and Mrs Churchill arrived they were escorted down the long concrete stairway to the operations room one hundred feet below ground. Park commented that he did not know if there would be any enemy activity; for the moment all was quiet.

NEAR ABBEVILLE, FRANCE, 10.40 A.M. Alois Lindmayr's formation was in trouble. During their climb to attack altitude, the Dorniers passed through a cloud layer that proved thicker than expected. The navigator in one of the bombers, Feldwebel Theordor Rehm, described what happened:

> In cloud the visibility was so bad one could see only the flight leader's plane a few metres away. In our bomber four pairs of eyes strained to keep the aircraft in sight as its ghostly shape disappeared and reappeared in the alternating darkness and light. One moment it was clearly visible, menacingly large and near; then suddenly it would disappear from view, in the same place but shrouded in billowing vapour. At the same time we also scanned the sky around for other aircraft, ready to bellow a warning if there was a risk of collision. After several anxious minutes that felt like an eternity, we emerged from cloud at about 3,500 metres [11,000 feet]. Around us were the familiar shapes of Dorniers spread over a large area in ones, twos and threes. Our attack formation had been shattered.

Above cloud, the leading Dornier flew a series of wide orbits to allow the others to re-form behind it. The move imposed a delay of ten minutes on the attack schedule. Two of the bombers failed to rejoin the formation and returned to base.

UXBRIDGE, 11.00 A.M. Sitting in one of the galleries overlooking the operations room, the Prime Minister had given express instructions that the staff were not to behave any differently from normal on his account. Dominating the floor of the operations room was a huge plotting table bearing a gridded map of the southern half of England and northern Europe, covering an area bounded by Lincoln in the north, Antwerp in the east, Le Havre in the south and Exeter in the west. For the moment there was little activity. Apart from markers representing the lone German reconnaissance planes and the sections of British fighters sent after them, the table was bare. Occasionally a WAAF would push her wooden rake across the table to re-position a marker, but otherwise everything was quiet.

Those WAAFs on duty in the plotting room with nothing to do were left to their own devices. Some knitted, others read books or magazines, yet others talked quietly with colleagues. Aircraft-woman Vera Saies sat beside the plotting table writing to her parents, her earphones pushed to a position of comfort on her head.

At 11.04 a.m. the first of the German aircraft rose within view of the Chain Home radar station near Dover. The report of forty-plus aircraft in the Calais–Boulogne area was flashed to the Fighter Command filter room at Stanmore Park north of London, where the force was marked on the plotting table there and compared against known movements by RAF aircraft. The latter was the merest formality; no formation of British planes could have appeared so unexpectedly, or survived for long, in such an area. The plot was immediately designated 'hostile' and a WAAF broadcast the details to group and sector operations rooms throughout Fighter Command.

The remote voice in her headphones immediately parted Vera Saies from her letter, and as she thrust it to one side she pulled her earphones on firmly and called for an assistant to make up a marker block with the appropriate figures. When it arrived she pushed it with her rake into position on the map table.

GAP GRIS NEZ, 11.04 A.M. In his Messerschmitt 109, Ober-feldwebel Robert Olejnik orbited with the rest of his section at 16,000 feet. Around him were some thirty other planes of Fighter Geschwader 3, assigned to provide close escort for the bombers they were scheduled to meet. Occasionally he glanced anxiously to the south, but the Dornier formation was nowhere to be seen. London was eighty miles away, near the limit of the single-engined fighters' reach when they had to zig-zag to stay close to the bombers. *And* they needed to arrive there with sufficient fuel to do battle with enemy fighters. Each minute the Messerschmitts spent circling at the French coast would be one minute less they spent with the bombers over England.

Like many a German aircrewman, Olejnik suspected that the enemy had warning of the raids long before they crossed the coast of England. He was of course right – the marker Vera Saies had moved into place on the plotting table at Uxbridge represented his and other waiting Messerschmitts being watched on radar.

At last the delayed formation of Dorniers hove into sight. The sun glinting off the wings and canopies of the bombers gave no clue to the problems they had encountered on the way.

UXBRIDGE, 11.04 A.M. From his vantage point overlooking the plotting table, Winston Churchill watched a new marker indicating thirty-plus hostiles being pushed across the map before coming to rest near Calais. The marker represented Alois Lindmayr's Dorniers, ten minutes late and now about to pick up their escorts.

Wing Commander Lord Willoughby de Broke, Keith Park's senior fighter controller, also watched the hostile markers advancing across the plotting map. At this stage he had no way of knowing which plots represented bombers and which represented enemy fighters. Fighters flying alone he could ignore; bombers had to be intercepted, preferably before they reached their target. Before he committed his fighters, de Broke knew he had to strike a careful balance. On the one hand he had to scramble them early enough to climb to height and get into a good attacking position; but on the other he had to avoid scrambling them too early lest the fighters run short of fuel before they met the enemy. He told the author:

> The Group controller's job was like a glorified game of chess, only infinitely more exciting and responsible as so much was at stake. The Germans would frequently put up 'spoof' raids with the deliberate intention of 'foxing' our controllers, so that squadrons were ordered to patrol lines only to find that the 'plots' faded away as the enemy aircraft dispersed back to their bases in northern France. Our squadrons then had to land and refuel and, sensing this, the Germans would follow their 'spoof' raid pretty quickly with a genuine one, which necessitated putting up fresh squadrons to meet it while the others were refuelling.

Park excused himself from the Prime Minister and walked to the main control gallery to join de Broke. There was a brief discussion, then, as a preliminary move, Park told one of his assistants to scramble a couple of squadrons of Spitfires from Biggin Hill.

During the next ten minutes markers representing three separate forces of hostile aircraft appeared on the plotting table at Uxbridge. The force was assessed at 100-plus aircraft and on this occasion the radar operators' 'guestimate' was reasonably accurate. The markers represented the twenty-five Dorniers and their supporting fighters: a Gruppe of about thirty Me 109s providing close escort, another Gruppe providing extended cover and a third Gruppe to fly ahead of the force on a 'free hunt' for enemy fighters. Altogether there were about 120 German planes airborne.

Park and de Broke had observed the pattern develop several times before. This looked like the start of yet another major thrust against London. Still the composition of the enemy force was unknown. If it comprised only Messerschmitts and was intended to draw British fighters into action, that was just how it could be expected to look. It was a risk Park had to accept. Reading from the state board on the wall beyond the map table, he directed his staff to scramble nine more squadrons.

A few clipped orders, passed by telephone in subdued tones, were all that was necessary to send the Spitfires and Hurricanes into the air. Like so many ant hills kicked into life by some huge invisible boot, the airfields at Northolt, Kenley and Debden, Castle Camps, Hornchurch, Hendon and Martlesham Heath became scenes of feverish activity until the last of the required fighters had left the ground.

HENDON AIRFIELD, NORTH LONDON, 11.15 A.M. For Sergeant Ray Holmes, a Hurricane pilot with No. 504 Squadron, this was supposed to be a rest period. Having been on alert since dawn, his unit had been stood down half an hour earlier. Now he was luxuriating in a much-needed bath at the Sergeants' Mess. Suddenly there was a bang on the door and someone shouted to him to get dressed and be quick about it – the squadron had been recalled to immediate readiness.

Holmes jumped from the bath and, without drying himself,

pulled on a blue sports shirt and uniform trousers. Then, bare-foot and clutching his socks, he galloped to the truck waiting outside the Mess. He ran as if his life depended on it, because it might – if the squadron was ordered to scramble, every thirty seconds' delay in getting airborne could mean 1,000 feet it would not have if it encountered enemy fighters before reaching the top of climb. Urged on by his impatient colleagues, Holmes leapt into the back of the vehicle, which then accelerated for the far side of the airfield where the squadron's Hurricanes were dispersed. Sitting on the floor Holmes pulled socks over still-wet feet with one hand, struggling to brace himself with the other as the vehicle lurched round corners.

The truck squealed to a halt beside the fighters' dispersal area and the pilots jumped to the ground, just as loudspeakers bellowed the scramble order. Holmes sprinted to the squadron hut, pulled on his flying boots, grabbed his life jacket and, donning it on the way, ran to his Hurricane. He clambered into the cockpit and, while the mechanic helped him do up his parachute and seat straps, he reached down to start the engine. It burst into life with a roar, as Squadron Leader John Sample led the procession of hump-backed fighters from the dispersal area and headed purposefully to the downwind end of the grass airfield. Holmes waved away the chocks, pushed forward his throttle and followed the others. Meanwhile Sample had started his take-off run. In ones and twos the rest of the Hurricanes chased after him. The leader circled the airfield to allow the squadron to assemble in formation behind him, then turned south-east and climbed for his assigned patrol area over Maidstone.

STRAIT OF DOVER, 11.20 A.M. While Park's fighter squadrons clawed for altitude and made for their assigned patrol areas, the Dorniers of Bomber Geschwader 76 left the French coast heading north-west, passing through 14,000 feet in a shallow climb. The Messerschmitt 109s of the close-cover and open-cover forces were in position around the bombers, while those of the free-hunting force sped out in front.

DOVER, 11.20 A.M. As the German formations set out from France, Air-Raid Warning Red was issued for south-eastern Kent. At Dover the sirens sounded, followed soon afterwards by those at Folkestone, Deal and Hythe. In each town the anti-aircraft gunners and civil defence units were stood to for action. Most people took to the shelters, but others, braver or more ignorant of the risks, continued with their tasks but kept a wary eye to the sky.

UXBRIDGE, 11.20 A.M. By the seventh week of the Battle of Britain, Air Vice-Marshal Park had developed his defensive tactics to a fine art. If this was yet another attack on London, he knew that the Messerschmitt 109 force would be operating near the limit of its radius of action.

The essence of good tactics is to exploit an enemy's weaknesses, and Park planned to fight the forthcoming battle in three phases. In the first phase, to begin shortly after the German formations crossed the coast, the Spitfire squadrons on the forward patrol lines would go into action. If possible these fighters were to engage the bombers and break up their formation. But if the escorting Messerschmitts prevented this and dogfights developed, that too would serve Park's purpose. It might draw some of the escorts away from the bombers, leaving them more vulnerable to British squadrons attacking later. It would also force the German fighters to fly at full throttle, burning fuel four times faster than in the cruise.

During the second phase, extending over the next ten to fifteen minutes as the raiders continued towards the capital, four or five pairs of Hurricane squadrons were to be fed into the action from different directions to try and reach the bombers. Again, if these squadrons became embroiled with the Messerschmitts, the latter would be forced to use yet more fuel.

In the third and final phase of the engagement, the remaining fighter squadrons would be hurled into the fray immediately in front of London. By then, Park hoped, the Me 109s would be short of fuel and ammunition.

Although he had not committed all his own squadrons, Air Vice-Marshal Park was already asking for help from neighbouring fighter Groups. At his request No. 10 Group scrambled a squadron of Spitfires and sent it east to patrol over the Windsor area. Also, the No. 12 Group controller at Watnall near Nottingham ordered the 'Big Wing' of three squadrons of Hurricanes and two of Spitfires to scramble and move into position over north London. For the first time, the tactic of employing so many fighters *en masse* against a German formation was to be tested in action.

DUXFORD AIRFIELD, 11.25 A.M. Squadron Leader Douglas Bader and the units assigned to the Big Wing had been at readiness throughout the morning. Despite the amputation of both legs following a pre-war flying accident, Bader had shown that with a pair of artificial legs he could handle a fighter better than most pilots. On receipt of the scramble order Bader led his three squadrons of Hurricanes into the air, following the sequence rehearsed several times previously. He later told the author: 'The fighters were dispersed around the perimeter of the airfield. When the order came to scramble, we [242 Squadron] taxied out and took off as a squadron, almost in line abreast. As we got airborne 310 (Czech Squadron] was moving to the take-off point, followed by 302 [Polish Squadron]. Once I was off the ground I curved on to a southerly heading for London and the others followed. No time was wasted in forming up. We just turned on to course and climbed, getting into formation as we did so.'

As the Hurricanes left Duxford, twenty Spitfires from Nos 19 and 611 Squadrons from nearby Fowlmere joined the formation. In the climb the higher performance Spitfires matched the 140 m.p.h. forward speed of the Hurricanes, but ascended more steeply. Again, that was how it had been rehearsed; when his formation met the enemy, Bader wanted the two Spitfire squadrons to be 5,000 feet above the Hurricanes, in position to protect the latter from the Messerschmitts. The thirty-five Hurricanes and twenty Spitfires had taken off and formed up in good time. It remained to be seen whether the powerful but unwieldy force could be brought into contact with a German bomber formation.

DOVER, 11.31 A.M. The spearhead of the German force, the Messerschmitt 109s assigned to the free-hunting role, crossed the coast of Kent and headed inland. Their task was to disrupt British fighter attacks before they reached the bombers. As they passed Dover the Messerschmitts were engaged by the port's defences, twelve 3.7-in. and two 3-in. guns belonging to 75th Heavy Anti-Aircraft Regiment, Royal Artillery. The gunners loosed off several salvoes but none of the fighters was hit.

Fighter Command Initial Scrambles, 11.05 to 11.25 a.m.

Time Airborne	Sector	Disposition
No. 11 Group		
11.05	Biggin Hill	Nos 72 and 92 Squadrons, 20 Spitfires, to Canterbury at 25,000 feet.
11.15	Northolt	Nos 229 and 303 Squadrons, 24 Hurricanes, to Biggin Hill at 15,000 feet.
	Kenley	Nos 253 and 501 Squadrons, 23 Hurricanes, to Maidstone at 15,000 feet.
	Debden	No. 17 Squadron (Debden) and No. 73 (Castle Camps), 21 Hurricanes, to Chelmsford at 15,000 feet.
11.20	Hornchurch	No. 603 Squadron, 12 Spitfires, to Dover at 20,000 feet.
	North Weald	No. 257 Squadron (Martlesham Heath) and No. 504 (Hendon), 20 Hurricanes, to Maidstone at 15,000 feet.
No. 10 Group		
11.20	Middle Wallop	No. 609 Squadron, 13 Spitfires, to Brooklands–Windsor area at 15,000 feet.
No. 12 Group		
11.25	Duxford	Nos 242, 302 and 310 Squadron, 35 Hurricanes; Nos 19 and 611 Squadrons (Fowlmere), 20 Spitfires. 'Big Wing' to Hornchurch at 20,000 feet.

Six minutes, about eighteen miles, behind the free-hunting Messerschmitts, the Dorniers of Bomber Geschwader 76 and their escorts crossed the coast near Folkestone at 16,000 feet and came under fire from the port's six 3-in. guns. Wilhelm Raab watched a cluster of cotton-wool puffs from the bursting shells appear suddenly to one side of his bomber. The Dorniers opened formation and, following their leader, began a 'flak waltz' that took them snaking across the sky to put the enemy gunners off their aim. Again, none of the planes was hit.

CALAIS-MARCK AIRFIELD, 11.36 A.M. As the Dorniers crossed the English coast, the remaining part of the German raiding force was taking off. Twenty-one Messerschmitt 109 fighter-bombers of the Lehr Geschwader 2, all carrying bombs under their bellies, climbed to the north-west in loose formation. Accompanying the fighter-bombers was a similar number of Messerschmitts without bombs, the escorts.

The Messerschmitt fighter-bombers were to deliver their nuisance raid on London a few minutes before the main raiding force reached the capital. Even encumbered by bombs, the Me 109s cruised about 90 m.p.h. faster than the Dorniers and would easily overtake the latter along the route.

THE ENTIRE GERMAN force assinged to the attack on London was now airborne and advancing on the target: 25 twin-engined bombers, 21 fighter-bombes and a covering force of about 150 Messerschmitts. It was a formidable assembly of air power that would take a lot of stopping. On this occasion, however, the defenders enjoyed support from a powerful if invisible ally.

As we have observed, even before the bombers left France their formation had been disrupted by unexpectedly thick cloud. Now the vagaries of the British weather were about to take a second swipe at the German plan. As the Dorniers advanced across Kent their navigators measured their ground speed by tracking the relative movement of landmarks through their bombsights. The routine operation brought a disconcerting discovery: the formation's rate of advance was much slower than planned, about 90 m.p.h. instead of the expected 180 m.p.h. Between 16,000 and 20,000 feet over south-east England that day there was a powerful 90 m.p.h. wind from the north-west. At such altitudes a wind of that strength is not unusual, but the German meteorologists had made no mention of it at their briefings that morning. Thus, instead of the expected half-hour flight time from Cap Gris Nez to London, it was going to take about twice that long. With the delay incurred in reassembling formation over France, the Dorniers were going to be about forty minutes late at their target.

KENT, 11.36 A.M. Like a beach being submerged by an incoming tide, the area of south-east England under alert was growing steadily. Now Air-Raid Warning Red was in force to the line Rochester–Maidstone–Tunbridge Wells–Hastings.

At the village of Staplehurst, to the south of Maidstone, 21-year-old Freda Tomlin was walking to church with her mother and two sisters. The distant sirens did nothing to dis-

Fighter Command's Second Wave of Scrambles, 11.38 to 11.42 a.m.

Time	Sector	Disposition
Airborne		
No. 11 Group		
11.38	North Weald	Nos 46 and 249 Squadrons, 20 Hurricanes, to south London.
11.40	Northolt	Nos 1 (Canadian) and 605 Squadrons, 24 Hurricanes, to Kenley at 15,000 feet.
	Hornchurch	No. 41 Squadron, 12 Spitfires, to Gravesend at 20,000 feet.
11.42	Biggin Hill	No. 66 Squadron, 10 Spitfires, to intercept.
No. 11 Group Fighting Reserve, 11.42 a.m.		
	Tangmere	Nos 213, 607 and 602 Squadrons (32 Hurricanes, 15 Spitfires).
	Hornchurch	No. 222 Squadron (11 Spitfires).

suade the family from their devotions, for the air battles had become almost commonplace and previous ones had made no impact on the village. There was no reason to believe that this one would be any different.

UXBRIDGE, 11.36 A.M. No. 11 Group's operations room was a hive of activity as WAAF plotters surrounding the map table continually adjusted the markers representing friendly and hostile formations. The picture had the appearance of yet another full-blooded German attack on the capital, and, after a further brief conference with de Broke, Park ordered six more squadrons to scramble.

At 11.42 a.m., when the last of these aircraft left the ground, Fighter Command had twenty-three squadrons airborne – 254 Spitfires and Hurricanes. Nobody on either side could know, but the defending fighters outnumbered the German force by five to four and the escorting Me 109s by five to three. In achieving this favourable ratio Keith Park had contrived to retain a fighting reserve of four squadrons of Spitfires and Hurricanes on the ground. If the action took an unexpected turn, these too would be scrambled.

SOUTH LONDON, 11.45 A.M. As the approaching enemy force came within forty miles of the capital, the sirens along the southern outskirts began to blare out their undulating note of warning. Two minutes later those in central London followed suit. Again many of the citizens made their way to the shelters, while others decided to continue with what they were doing and take their chances.

When the sirens sounded in Kennington, 33-year-old lorry driver Walter Chesney and his wife were travelling by bus to Petticoat Lane market. The vehicle was approaching the Oval underground station. In accordance with the now-established procedure, the driver stopped the bus and the conductor ordered all passengers to get off and suggested they take shelter. The journey would be resumed when the all-clear sounded.

A few hundred yards north-west of the Chesneys, in Harleyford Road, ten-year-old Ron McGill and his mother were on their way home after visiting relatives. There was still some way to go, so the mother grabbed her son's hand and the pair quickened their pace, hastening along the rapidly emptying street.

About a mile south-west of the McGills, at Odger Street, Battersea, 33-year-old butcher Albert Brown was visiting his widowed mother when the siren sounded. Despite his appeals she refused to go with him to the nearby shelter. He felt he had to remain with her in the sitting room, and hoped this was yet another false alarm.

A mile to the north of the Browns, at Gatliff Road, Chelsea, draughtsman Jack Hill, 23, became an air raid warden when the warning was sounded. He donned his steel helmet and strode to his post. His task was to watch for falling incendiary bombs, and endeavour to extinguish them before fires took hold.

Four hundred yards to the north of Hill, at Victoria coach station, chief engineer Reg Garman, 38, checked that everyone was out of the building. Then he switched off the electrical supply to the lifts and the boilers, and laid out the fire-fighting equipment for immediate use.

ASHFORD, 11.50 a.m. When Alois Lindmayr's Dorniers passed over the town, the formation of Messerschmitt fighter-bombers also heading for London was about fifteen miles behind, 4,000 feet higher and catching up fast. As the raiders droned deeper into enemy territory, their alert crews swept the skies for the first sign of reaction from the defenders.

It would not be long in coming. About ten miles north-east of

Positions of German Formations, and RAF Fighter Squadrons, at 11.50 a.m. when the Action Began.

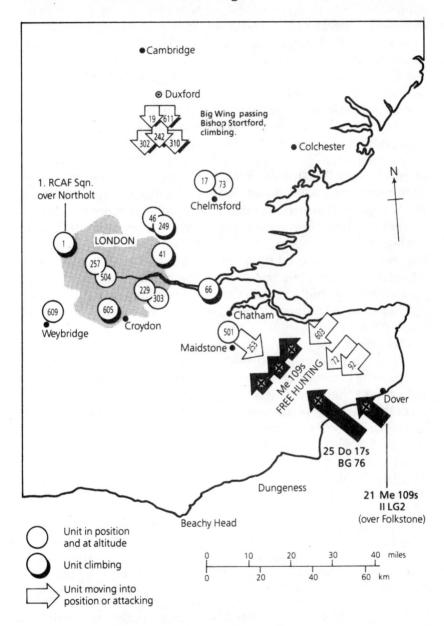

the German bombers, at 25,000 feet, Flight Lieutenant 'Pancho' Villa at the head of twenty Spitfires from Nos 72 and 92 Squadrons suddenly caught sight of the enemy formation, a swarm of midge-like specks almost stationary in the distance. Villa gave a brief radio call: 'Tennis Squadron, Tally Ho!' That told the other pilots he had the enemy in sight, and informed the ground controller at Biggin Hill that he would require no further assistance unless he asked for it.

Villa led his force in a sweeping turn to the left, closing rapidly on the enemy. As he did so he carefully quartered the sky for high-flying Messerschmitts. He saw none.

The two squadrons of Spitfires were 9,000 feet above the Dorniers and 3,000 feet above the highest of the escorting Messerschmitts. Altitude advantage was treasure to the fighter pilot, readily convertible into speed when the time came to pounce on the enemy. Swinging rapidly into position to attack the escorts, Villa ordered his fighters into line astern. Then the leading Spitfire pivoted on its right wing and arced into a dive. At measured intervals the rest of the fighters followed, as if performing a high-speed three-dimensional conga chain. Accelerating rapidly, the Spitfires bore down on their still unsuspecting foes.

Then from one of the Messerschmitts there came a sudden shouted warning call, and things happened fast and at rising tempo. The German fighter pilots pushed forward their throttles, abandoned their seemingly aimless zig-zagging and turned to meet their assailants. Escorts flying to the south and west of the formation turned to support their comrades. The sky became a confused mêlée of fighters twisting and turning to deliver attacks, or to avoid being attacked. The combat report by Sergeant William Rolls of No. 72 Squadron shows how quickly fortunes could change during an action of this sort:

> I saw an Me 109 coming down and it passed well over my head and appeared to be firing at the aircraft in front of me. As it climbed up again I climbed after it and at 200 yards I gave a burst of about 2 or 3 seconds from underneath it. I saw a big black patch appear and several small ones on the fuselage. I saw some tracer coming from behind me as well and in my mirror saw another Me 109 coming down at me. I evaded it and could not get round to fire at it because it climbed away. As there were about 20 more above with it, I decided to leave it.

During this skirmish Spitfires of No. 92 Squadron attempted to charge through to the Dorniers, but vigilant Messerschmitts blocked their way at each attempt.

Shortly afterwards, a dozen Spitfires of No. 603 Squadron joined the action and waded into the escorts. Pilot Officer Macphail singled out one of the Messerschmitts for attack: 'I turned and chased the enemy and got in a burst from astern. He turned to the left and I got another burst. The enemy rolled on his back with pieces flying off his machine and dived into the corner of a small wood a few miles south of Detling aerodrome and burst into flames.' Oberleutnant Rudolph Schmidt of Fighter Geschwader 53 jumped from the stricken fighter, but his parachute failed to open.

The escorts were now fully committed, and twenty-three Hurricanes of Nos 253 and 501 Squadrons were able to deliver a head-on attack on the Dorniers without interference. From the nose of his bomber Theodor Rehm watched the British fighters coming in. 'Their thrusting attack took them right through our formation. Manning the nose gun, I dared not open fire for fear of hitting our own aircraft. But the Hurricanes flashing close past us did not do much firing either, and we came out of the attack unscathed.' The Dorniers' rear gunners loosed off bursts at each Hurricane as it came past, to speed it on its way.

From another of the Dorniers, Wilhelm Raab also observed the engagement. 'They came in fast, getting bigger and bigger. As usual when under attack from fighters, we closed into tight formation to concentrate our defensive fire,' he recalled. 'Four Hurricanes scurried through our formation. Within seconds they were past. Then more black specks emerged from the bank of cloud in front, rapidly grew larger and flashed through our formation. They were trying to split us up, but neither attack had any success. Our formation remained intact.'

Afterwards the Hurricanes attempted to re-form for a second attack on the bombers, but became involved in dogfights with the escorts in which No. 501 Squadron lost two aircraft. Pilot Officer van den Hove d'Ertsenrijck, a Belgian, was killed when his fighter was hit by several cannon shells and blew up in mid-air. Squadron Leader Harry Hogan was attacked by an Me 109 from behind, his radiator was hit and he was forced to shut down his engine. The fighter went into a spin but Hogan recovered and made a wheels-down landing in a meadow near Sevenoaks.

Also at this time a further twenty-four Hurricanes (Nos 229 and 303 Squadrons) joined the brawl around the German bombers. High over the patchwork landscape of Kent the opposing fighters wove crazy patterns across the sky. The action devolved into a series of scrappy combats, in which neither side gained the advantage.

STAPLEHURST, NOON. In All Saints' Church the Reverend Alfred Walker was delivering his sermon, unmoved by the battle in progress overhead. Freda Tomlin, one of those in the congregation, later commented: 'We could hear the machine-gun fire during the sermon, but by then this was quite common. The vicar continued speaking and we just sat there and listened.'

About a mile to the north of the church, Police Constable Bill Albon was walking his beat beside Staplehurst station. He too could hear the distant scream of aero engines and the crackle of gunfire, but a layer of cloud concealed what was happening above the village.

Leutnant Hans Bertel of Fighter Geschwader 52 was one of those involved in the action taking place above Albon: 'There were four or five Hurricanes in the dogfight, and about the same number of Me 109s,' he recalled. 'I had my gunsight on one of the Hurricanes and was about to pull the trigger. Then there came a sudden hard knock, and my Messerschmitt fell into a spin. Another plane had collided wth my tail. I tried to pull out of the spin, but I had no control over my rudder or elevators. The motor was excellent, the wings were excellent, but the tail was useless!'

The world twirling around him, Bertel decided to abandon the Messerschmitt. But the plane was in a violent spin and powerful G forces pinioned his arms and prevented him reaching the lever to jettison the canopy. As the fighter built up speed in the dive, however, the rate of rotation slowed. The G forces fell as the pilot's adrenaline level rose, until finally he was able to grab the lever. A sharp tug and the canopy was gone. 'I must have been going down very fast, because outside it sounded like a thunderstorm. I released my seat straps and was hurled clear of the aircraft. My first thought was "Don't open the parachute yet or it will be torn to shreds!" After a short wait I pulled the ripcord and the parachute popped open.' Hanging from his straps Bertel surveyed the scene around but could see nothing of his Messerschmitt. Then, far below, he noticed a spinning Hurricane vanish into cloud. He was sure it was the plane that had collided with his.

Standing beside Staplehurst station, Bill Albon was trying without success to sort out the profusion of unfamiliar sounds coming from above. Then a fast-revving aircraft engine drowned out everything else, seemingly coming straight for him. Seconds later a Hurricane emerged from cloud and plunged into the ground at a shallow angle, less than a hundred yards from the startled policeman. Shedding pieces, the plane bounced over the railway line and smashed through a couple of railway buildings, before coming to rest in a cloud of steam and dust on the far side of the station. A junior booking clerk was killed and the station master received severe head injuries. The lifeless body of the plane's Belgian pilot, Pilot Officer Georges Doutrepont, was still inside what was left of the cockpit.

Parts of the Hurricane smashed into the general store beside the station belonging to Margaret Nolan, a widow in her fifties. 'The first I heard was a terrible crash,' she afterwards recounted. 'Pieces of machinery smashed through the shop window close to me and a piece of petrol tank flew past my head. Indeed things were flying all around me, but I never got a scratch. I dashed into my living room and it was in flames. The wheel of the plane was burning there and a young man threw it into the street, or the place would have burnt down.'

Bertel's Messerschmitt crashed just outside Staplehurst. The German pilot emerged from cloud on his parachute. 'It was a Sunday and below me I could see a lot of people out walking, and children playing ball. Then they began to notice me coming down on my parachute, it was amazing as the heads of the people changed colour as they turned their faces to look at me.' Bertel landed beside a hedge and was immediately taken into custody by a couple of Home Guardsmen, the first of sixty-three of his countrymen to be captured that day.

ABOVE MAIDSTONE, NOON. Several of the British fighters had expended their ammunition and now broke out of the action. For a few minutes the fighting slackened, having claimed the destruction of three Hurricanes and at least two

Messerschmitts. None of the Dorniers had suffered serious damage and their formation remained intact. Could it be, some of the more optimistic Germans wondered, that they had already broken through the British defences?

The Dorniers passed over West Malling airfield, defended by a couple of elderly 3-in. anti-aircraft guns. The gunners banged off about thirty rounds at the enemy force, but to no effect.

Also at this time the Messerschmitt 109 fighter-bombers, flying at 23,000 feet, swept over the formation of Dorniers. Cruising at 270 m.p.h. into the 90 m.p.h. headwind, the Messerschmitts were making 180 m.p.h. over the ground – twice the speed of the twin-engined bombers.

NORTH OF SEVENOAKS, 12.03 P.M. Again the air fighting flared up, as four fresh squadrons of Hurricanes (Nos 1 Canadian, 46, 249 and 605) closed on the lower of the two German forces.

The Canadians tried to force their way through to the Dorniers, but several sections of Messerschmitts from Fighter Geschwader 53, led by Hauptmann Hans-Karl Mayer, moved to head them off. Flying Officer Deane Nesbitt afterwards reported: 'We were attacked by some Me 109s from above and up-sun and had partially turned to meet the attack. The formation of the squadron broke up and the engagement developed into a dogfight. An Me 109 crossed in front of me and I fired a long burst at close range.' Nesbitt's colleagues saw the Messerschmitt go down in flames. The pilot, Oberleutnant Julius Haase, was killed.

Moments later cannon shells rammed into Nesbitt's own fighter. The cockpit filled with smoke and the Hurricane started to fall out of control. Nesbitt's assailant, Unteroffizier Wilhelm Ghesla, later wrote: 'Shortly before reaching London we became involved in a dogfight with 12 Spitfires [sic] that tried to attack the bombers. I saw one of the Spitfires chasing a Messerschmitt 109. Unseen by the enemy I positioned myself behind the Spitfire, closed to about 80 metres and opened fire. The machine trailed smoke and soon afterwards its pilot bailed out.' Obviously Ghesla was one of those Germans to whom 'Spitfire' was synonymous with 'British fighter'. Nesbitt landed by parachute with minor injuries.

While the German escorts were thus occupied, Flight Lieutenant Archie McKellar led the twelve Hurricanes of No. 605 Squadron in a snap attack on the Dorniers. Some of his pilots claimed hits, but still the bombers held formation and continued determinedly towards the capital.

SOUTH-EAST LONDON, 12.05 P.M. As the defenders concentrated on the Dorniers and their immediate escorts, the fighter-bombers of Lehr Geschwader 2 were allowed to reach London unchallenged. The high flyers looked like yet another German free-hunting patrol, and RAF pilots had learned the hard way to leave those well alone. Only one defending pilot, Pilot Officer Gunning of No. 46 Squadron, reported seeing that part of the raiding force. He spoke of a force of Me 109s that passed over him, but they 'did not appear to attempt to attack anyone below'. The Messerschmitts' pilots had orders to engage enemy fighters only if they were directly threatened. In this instance, each side preferred to avoid the other.

When the fighter-bombers reached the city, their leader, Hauptmann Otto Weiss, banked his aircraft steeply and picked out one of the railway stations below. Then, with his two wing-men in close formation on either side, he pushed his Messerschmitt into a 45-degree dive and lined up on the target. After a descent through about 3,000 feet he released his bomb, as did his wing-men, and the three fighter-bombers pulled out of their dives. The other Messerschmitts attacked in a similar manner. Their task completed, the fighter-bombers turned for home. None was approached by British fighters.

At Broxholm Road, West Norwood, 28-year-old meat salesman Frank Skinner and his wife were discussing whether to put their baby son in the cellar for safety. The sirens had sounded twenty minutes earlier but it seemed nothing was happening outside. Then came a loud bang and the house shook. Earlier Daisy Skinner had washed the linoleum on the dining room floor, and opened the windows so that it would dry quickly. About a second after the first bang came a second, much closer, as the chimney from the next house crashed to the ground beside an open window. A cloud of brick dust engulfed the room, ruining the earlier work. 'Look at my clean floor!' she blurted.

After putting Daisy and the baby in the cellar, Frank Skinner went outside to see what had happened. He did not need to look far. The house three doors along his terrace had suffered a direct hit. The front of the building had been blown off and debris was strewn across the road. But the rear of the house remained standing, the insides of the upstairs rooms exposed to view from the street.

Police and a rescue team were quickly on the scene, and began clearing away rubble to free the two women and a young child trapped in the cellar. All three were brought out with minor cuts and bruises.

Given the crude method of bomb-aiming, the Messerschmitts' attack could not have been anything but indiscriminate. Bombs were scattered over a wide area of Penge, Dulwich, Streatham and Lambeth, and only four came down near military targets. Three 110-pounders landed beside the railway track near Birkbeck station. One failed to go off, preventing a start to repair work until it was made safe. Services were halted between Beckenham Junction, Norwood Junction and Crystal Palace stations. Another bomb, probably aimed at West Norwood station, landed beside the Telephone Manufacturing Company's factory at Streatham and it too failed to explode; 2,500 workers on the Sunday afternoon shift had to be sent home and production ceased until the bomb was dealt with. At Brixton Hill a bomb set fire to a gas main and blocked the thoroughfare. The bomb that landed near Frank Skinner's home had probably been aimed at the entrance of a rail tunnel about two-hundred yards away. The worst incident was at Bourdon Road near Penge station, where one person was killed and eight injured.

LEWISHAM, 12.07 P.M. Although there had been some spirited attacks on the German bombers, the latter arrived over the outskirts of London without loss. Their formation was intact, except for Oberleutnant Robert Zehbe's Dornier which had engine trouble and was trailing half a mile behind the rest. The German escorts had done their work well, having blocked most of the attempts by Spitfires and Hurricanes to get through to the bombers.

Now, however, the Dorniers' forty-minute delay in reaching the target had its inevitable result. The Messerschmitt 109 escorts had taken off punctually at their briefed times, and worked to a tight schedule that allowed little latitude for changes of plan. Moreover, Air Vice-Marshal Park's tactic of feeding squadrons into the action throughout the raiders' approach had set up running fights that forced the German fighters to fly at full throttle for long periods and ate into their fuel reserves. Thus, when they reached London's eastern outskirts, many of the Me 109s had sufficient fuel only for their return flight. In twos and fours, escorts started to break away from the action and point their snouts to the south-east.

Now the action was about to enter its third phase, for Park's controllers had concentrated six squadrons (Nos 17, 41, 66, 73, 257 and 504) over the capital itself. Also, heading there from the north and the west, were a further six squadrons from neighbouring Groups (No. 609 from No. 10 Group, and Nos 19, 242, 302, 310, and 611 from No. 12 Group). A total of 127 Spitfires and Hurricanes were about to clash with about one-fifth their number of German bombers and a rapidly dwindling force of escorts.

BATTERSEA, 12.07 P.M. Standing on the balcony of his mother's flat in Odger Street, Albert Brown noticed a formation of aircraft high in the sky and coming towards him. Returning to the sitting room he renewed his efforts to get his mother to go to the shelter with him, but in vain. She had also seen the planes, and Albert, trying to humour her, insisted they were British: 'They must be ours,' he said. 'Theirs wouldn't come over here at lunch time, would they?' The question was answered as soon as it was uttered, as smaller planes began diving into the formation and a stutter of machine-gun fires was heard above the drone of engines. Mother and son stood rooted to the spot.

SIXTEEN THOUSAND FEET OVER BRIXTON, 12.08 P.M. With the bomber formation in clear view, several anti-aircraft gun batteries opened fire on the raiders. Then, one by one, the batteries were ordered to cease fire as yet more British fighters moved into the area. Holding his Dornier straight and level for the bomb run, Wilhelm Raab noticed what looked like a swarm of small flies emerge from behind one of the clouds ahead. 'Of course they weren't flies. It was yet more British fighters, far in the distance but closing rapidly. I counted ten before I had to give up and concentrate on holding formation.'

Piloting the nearest 'small fly', Squadron Leader John Sample led twenty Hurricanes of Nos 504 and 257 Squadrons in to attack. Ahead he could see the Dorniers clearly, silhouetted

47

above the cloud tops. 'As we converged I saw that there were about twenty of them and it looked as though it was going to be a nice party, for the other squadrons of Hurricanes and Spitfires also turned to join in,' he later wrote. 'By the time we reached a position near the bombers we were over London. We had gained a little height on them, too, so when I gave the order to attack we were able to dive on them from their right.'

To Raab and many of the Germans, it seemed that their enemy had cleverly waited until the Messerschmitts turned back before delivering the main fighter attack. The truth was more prosaic: Sample and the other British squadron commanders were merely following orders from ground controllers ignorant of the Dorniers' immediate predicament. The fact that there were no escorts near the bombers was a lucky break for the fighter pilots, but those preparing to engage the Dorniers knew that this could change in an instant: Messerschmitts had a nasty habit of turning up at the most inconvenient time. Everyone kept a careful lookout.

Sample picked out one of the Dorniers in the formation and closed on it, firing a long burst. The rest of the Hurricanes in his squadron followed. Then Flight Lieutenant Peter Brothers led in the Hurricanes of No. 257 Squadron. After the initial firing pass, the fighters split up and curved tightly to get behind the bombers for further attacks.

At the rear of the Dornier formation, Feldwebel Rolf Heitsch and his crew waited for a chance to use their 'secret weapon' – the flame-thrower mounted in the rear fuselage. The radio operator reported that a British fighter was closing in from astern; its pilot was about to receive his baptism of fire – literally.

The British pilot in mortal danger was Ray Holmes, still damp under his clothes after the hastily curtailed bath. He lined up behind Heitsch's bomber, opened fire from 400 yards and saw his tracer rounds streaking towards the enemy plane. Then his windscreen was suddenly covered in sticky black oil that blotted out everything in front. In action the bomber's flame-thrower proved miserably inadequate for its intended task. The oil had burned well during tests at low altitude, but in the rarefied air at 16,000 feet the weapon produced only a short plume of flame less than 100 yards long. Most of the oil failed to ignite and some had sprayed over the Hurricane.

Unaware of the dreadful fate intended for him, Holmes

waited for the airflow to clear his windscreen. The panels changed from opaque to translucent, then he became aware of the blurred silhouette of the German bomber rapidly growing in front of him. With no room to bank or climb to avoid the enemy plane, Holmes pushed the nose of the Hurricane down sharply. Thrust hard against his straps by the negative G forces, he watched the belly of the Dornier pass close over the top of his canopy. Then he was clear.

By the end of the encounter Heitsch's Dornier was in serious trouble. A burst of machine-gun fire, perhaps that fired by Holmes before his windscreen was obscured, had wrecked the bomber's starboard engine. The German pilot feathered the propeller and struggled to hold the aircraft straight during the bombing run. British fighters were charging through the formation from all directions.

Meanwhile, straggling behind the main formation, Robert Zehbe's Dornier came under attack from several fighters. Pilot Officers Cochrane and North of No. 257 Squadron fired long bursts into the Dornier, as did Flying Officer Royce and Pilot Officer Rook of No. 504 Squadron. The bomber took terrible punishment and two of the crew were either dead or seriously wounded. Zehbe ordered the two others to bale out, then he set the bomber on autopilot and followed them.

Things were bad for Bomber Geschwader 76, and they were about to get worse. At this moment Squadron Leader Douglas Bader's 'Big Wing' had arrived over the capital, with fifty-five fighters. The three Hurricane squadrons were at 25,000 feet, the two of Spitfires were 2,000 feet higher and up-sun to block expected counter-attacks from German fighters. Flight Lieutenant Bob Oxspring of No. 66 Squadron was one of several No. 11 Group pilots heartened by the sight of the new arrivals: 'I saw the formation of five squadrons coming from the north, Douglas Bader's Wing. I thought "This is great! Five squadrons, that's what we want!" It must have been devastating for the Germans to see that lot coming in all at once.'

It was indeed a devastating sight for those in the Dorniers. Later the size of Bader's force would swell with the telling; an official Luftwaffe report on the action noted: 'Over the target large formations of fighters (with up to eighty aircraft) intercepted'. Certainly *this* did not look like the final spasm of a Royal Air Force in its death throes. Meanwhile, the German crews were fighting their way through the last seconds of the bombing run. Wilhelm Raab observed: 'With the British fighters whizzing through our formation, the leading aircraft began releasing their bombs. My navigator shouted "Ziel!" and released ours.' Looking like the rungs of a ladder without sides, sticks of 110-pounders fell away from each bomber in the formation.

After bomb-release the Dorniers, each lighter by a ton, began a sweeping curve to the left. It would take the formation about a minute to swing through a semi-circle, but for Theodor Rehm that turn seemed to last for ever. His section of three Dorniers, on the outside of the turn near the rear of the formation, began to drop behind the rest.

Wheeling his squadrons above the enemy formation, Douglas Bader waited impatiently for the fighters already engaging the bombers to finish their attacks. The 'Big Wing' was still on trial and nobody would thank him if his fighters got in the way of those of No. 11 Group. Finally the way was clear, and later Bader wrote: 'Dived down with leading section in formation onto last section of 3 enemy aircraft. P/O Campbell took left-hand Do 17, I took middle one and Sub Lt Cork the right hand one, which had lost ground on outside of turn.'

Bader dived on the leading Dornier in the section and opened fire from 100 yards; he saw his rounds striking the target, then he over-shot and pulled away in a steep climb. Sub Lieutenant Dick Cork, a Fleet Air Arm pilot seconded to Fighter Command, fired a burst into the Dornier on the right. Pilot Officer Campbell attacked the Dornier on the left, Theodor Rehm's. The German navigator recalled: 'We could hear the patter of bullets striking our wings and fuselage, but somehow the motors kept going. Our pilot, Unteroffizier Hanke, pulled the bomber first to the left then to the right to make it difficult for the enemy fighters to hit us. Suddenly there was a loud crash as bullets smashed through the radio operator's window and wrecked the mounting of his machine gun. The radio operator received splinter wounds to the chin, I felt a hefty blow on the back, but our wounds were only minor.'

Now the fight around the bombers developed into a confused fracas, as three by three the rest of the fighters in the 'Big Wing' joined the action. 'The sky was full of Spitfires and Hurricanes, queuing up and pushing each other out of the way to get at the Dorniers which for once were outnumbered,' Bader later wrote.

The Area in Battersea London that was Bombed during the Noon Attack.

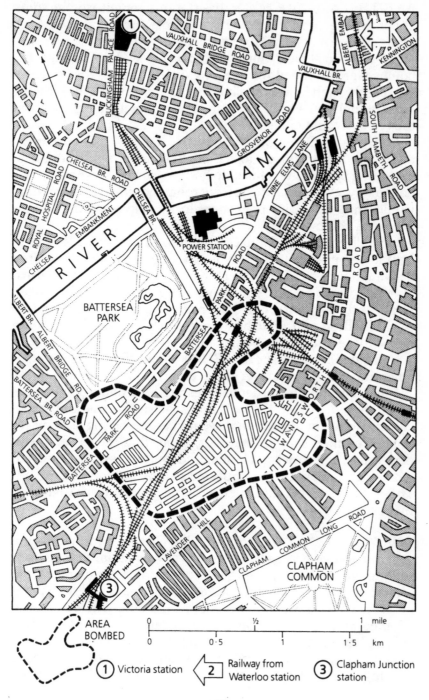

BATTERSEA, 12.10 P.M. Thirty seconds after release, the sticks of bombs began exploding in rows across the target area. Each plane's load of twenty 110-pounders carved a swathe of devastation about 500 yards long and 25 yards wide. Although the bombs were intended for the conglomeration of railway tracks passing through Battersea, abutting the tracks on each side were areas of high-density housing and it was inevitable that some of the bombs would fall here.

At the flat in Odger Street, Albert Brown had given up trying to get his mother to go to the shelter. Even at the sound of exploding bombs she refused to budge. 'So long as she stayed, I had to stay. We just sat in the front room, hoping that everything would miss us.' The pair were lucky. None of the bombs exploded nearby.

In Shellwood Road, housewife Winifred Kingman, 18, was in her kitchen preparing Sunday lunch. She had ignored the siren half an hour earlier, as there had been many false alarms. Suddenly there was a tremendous bang and a clatter of broken glass, and the front door disappeared. She grabbed her two small children and crouched protectively on the floor, as the house rocked under the blast of other explosions.

Constable Bernard Tucker, 33, was at Nine Elms police station when the raiders struck. With several colleagues he was in the canteen, awaiting the order to investigate the damage when the attack ended. Above the noise of explosions came the spine-chilling shriek of a bomb that seemed to be coming straight for them. The men sank to the floor, protecting their heads with their arms. The shriek got louder and louder then . . . it ceased. Obviously the bomb had impacted nearby but failed to go off. There was a sigh of relief, then a babble of nervous chatter filled the room.

DULWICH, 12.11 P.M. Although his Dornier had one engine shot out and he had been forced out of formation, Rolf Heitsch still thought he had a good chance of getting back to France. He was descending rapidly towards a bank of cloud, and once there he would be safe from the enemy fighters. But before the crippled bomber could reach cover it came under attack from several Hurricanes. Whenever a fighter approached, the radio operator triggered the flame-thrower and loosed off a geyser of burning oil. But the effect of the weapon was exactly the opposite of that intended. Instead of deterring attacking pilots, it gave the impression that the Dornier was about to catch fire. Sensing the chance of an easy kill, fighters were attracted to the diving bomber as moths to a candle. Later there would be oblique references to the flame-thrower in several RAF combat reports. Sergeant Robinson, No. 257 Squadron, noted that the Dornier 'caught fire in the rear'. Pilot Officer Campbell, No. 242 Squadron, noted: 'When I opened fire, smoke was observed issuing from the lower part of the fuselage of the enemy aircraft.' Sergeant Suidak, No. 302 Squadron, saw 'Black smoke pouring from the cockpit'. The same pilot noted that, as another Hurricane closed on the bomber, 'I saw the enemy aircraft catch fire *just before* the second Hurricane went in to attack.' During this part of the action none of the Dorniers caught fire in any of the ways mentioned, and it is clear that all these accounts referred to Heitsch's aircraft.

An accurate burst from one of the fighters severely wounded the Dornier's radio operator, ending the use of the 'secret weapon'. Heitsch felt his plane take more hits. A couple of Hurricanes roared close past the top of his canopy, then his remaining engine began to lose power.

CHELSEA, 12.11 P.M. While the main formation of bombers turned for home, hounded by scores of fighters, the Dornier abandoned by Robert Zehbe continued on auto-pilot on its north-westerly heading over the capital. And still the fighter attacks continued. Pilot Officers Cochrane and North of No. 257 Squadron fired further bursts into the Dornier, as did Flight Lieutenant Jeffries and Sergeant Hubacek of No. 310 Squadron and Flying Officer Ogilvie of No. 609 Squadron. Squadron Leader John Sample also engaged the lone bomber, and later wrote:

> I found myself below another Dornier which had white smoke coming from it. It was being attacked by two Hurricanes and a Spitfire, and was travelling north and turning slightly to the right. As I could not see anything else to attack at that moment I climbed above him and did a diving attack. Coming in to the attack, I noticed what appeared to be a red light shining in the rear gunner's cockpit, but when I got closer I realized I was looking right through the gunner's cockpit into the pilot's and observer's cockpit beyond. The 'red light' was a fire. I gave it a quick burst

and as I passed him on the right I looked in through the big glass nose of the Dornier. It was like a furnace inside.

After his encounter with Rolf Heitsch's bomber, Ray Holmes climbed back into the fight. He too noticed the solitary Dornier and ran in to attack it from head-on and slightly above. After a brief burst the Hurricane's guns fell silent; it was out of ammunition. Closing on the German plane at about 400 m.p.h., Holmes held his course. 'There was no time to weigh up the situation. His aeroplane looked so flimsy, I did not think of it as something solid and substantial. I just went on and hit the Dornier. I thought my aircraft would cut right through it, not allowing for the fact that his plane was as strong as mine,' Holmes later explained. With a crunch of tortured metal the Hurricane's port wing struck the bomber's port fin. 'There was a jolt when I hit him but not a big one. I thought nothing had happened to my plane, that I had got away with it.'

The effect of the collision on the Dornier was immediate and catastrophic. As if severed by some huge guillotine, the plane's fuselage broke into two and the entire tail unit detached itself. Lacking the stability provided by this vital appendage, the bomber responded like a child's see-saw after one of the riders jumps off. The nose dropped violently, imposing enormous forces on the wing. That structure immediately failed too, and on each side the outer wing snapped off as if it had been constructed from balsa wood and tissue paper. John Sample observed the incredible scene: 'The bomber did a forward somersault and then went into a spin . . . his wings broke off outboard of the engines, so that all that was left as the blazing aircraft fell was half a fuselage and the wing roots with the engines on their ends.'

The Dornier spun out of the sky like a boomerang returning to the hand that had thrown it. Still the plane carried its full complement of bombs, and now the savage G forces placed further irresistible demands on the already-weakened structure. Two 110-pounders and a container with sixteen incendiary bombs wrenched off their mountings and smashed their way through the side of the bomb bay.

Many hundreds of people watched the demise of the Dornier that Sunday afternoon. From her apartment in Eaton Square, the exiled Queen Wilhelmina of Holland watched it go down; later she would send a congratulatory telegram to the C.-in-C. Fighter Command. Other watchers took photographs of the bomber as it fell.

At the time Ron McGill was still being hastened by his mother along Harleyford Road, Kennington. 'We heard machine-gun fire above, and that made mum all the more desperate to get me home. She was tugging at the collar of my coat, while I kept trying to look up to see what was happening.' The young boy managed a quick upward glance and saw the sun glinting off pieces falling from the Dornier.

Meanwhile, Ray Holmes's Hurricane was also coming down fast. Following the collision the fighter continued on its trajectory. Then, slowly, as if poised on a distant fulcrum, its nose dropped and it banked steeply to the left. Holmes hauled on the stick to get the plane back on even keel but the controls had no effect. 'The nose fell, until I was going down in a vertical spiral dive. I was still trying to pull out when I entered cloud at 8,000 feet and lost my horizon and attitude. I realized that if I couldn't pull the plane out of the dive in a clear sky, I certainly was not going to pull it out when I was disorientated in cloud.'

Holmes slid back the canopy, undid his seat straps and scrambled out of the cockpit. The slipstream tore away his goggles, then, as he tumbled away, his right shoulder received a hefty knock. 'Apparently I struck the fin a glancing blow as I went past. I reached for the D-ring of my ripcord with my right hand, but because of the blow to my shoulder I had no strength in that arm. So I got hold of my right wrist with my left hand and yanked. That did the trick. The parachute opened with such a jerk that my flying boots came off.'

The first jetsam from the incident to reach the ground was the trio of bombs that had torn away from the stricken Dornier. One 110-pounder plunged into the roof of Buckingham Palace and smashed through a couple of floors before coming to rest in the bathroom of one of the royal apartments. The other 110-pounder, and the container with sixteen incendiary bombs, landed in the Palace grounds. The fuses of the two larger bombs had not been made 'live' and neither detonated. Some of the incendiary bombs ignited on hitting the ground, starting small grass fires which were quickly extinguished by the Palace fire watchers. The Royal Family was not in residence at the time.

Next to hit the ground was Ray Holmes's Hurricane. Diving almost vertically, the fighter was probably doing more than 400 m.p.h. when it plummeted into the road at the junction of Buckingham Palace Road and Pimlico Road, Chelsea. The engine, weighing about half a ton, smashed through the tarmac and into the soil beneath, demolishing a water main in the process. Reg Garman was descending the stairs at Victoria coach station when the plane impacted about a hundred yards away. 'I heard an almighty bang and the whole building shook. I thought a bomb had exploded nearby. When I got to the bottom of the stairs I looked outside and to my astonishment saw water cascading down Buckingham Palace Road from a broken main.' Apart from some pieces of twisted aluminium lying on the

Map of London showing where the different parts of the Dornier, and the Hurricane, came down after the collision, and the positions of Witnesses.

pavement there was little to be seen of the fighter. The rest was in the crater it had dug for itself.

Dangling from his parachute, Ray Holmes's main concern was where he might land. He feared that it would be on the expanse of railway tracks running south from Victoria station. 'I thought "Bloody Hell, those lines are electrified!" As my glance followed the rail track something caught my eye: the fuselage and inner wings of the Dornier, fluttering down like a leaf, about half a mile away. I didn't watch it hit the ground. I was getting awfully close to those electrified lines.'

Standing in the street beside Victoria coach station, Reg Garman also watched the dismembered Dornier coming down. 'It was the most amazing sight I have ever seen: A German bomber, its tail missing, sailing past overhead. It disappeared behind some buildings, then I heard the crash and a column of black smoke rose into the sky. The plane had crashed beside Victoria station, about 400 yards north of me.'

When the Dornier impacted, Ray Holmes was getting close to the ground. The north-easterly breeze carried him clear of the rail lines, but an inner city area contains innumerable perils for the descending parachutist. Next in his path lay a three-storey

---

Key: 1. Forecourt of Victoria Station, where the main part of the Dornier crashed.
2. Vauxhall Bridge Road, where the tail of the Dornier landed.
3. Buckingham Palace and Grounds, where two high explosive bombs and a canister of incendiary bombs from the Dornier landed.
4. Newburn Street, where an outer wing panel from the Dornier landed.
5. The Oval underground station, where the pilot of the Dornier landed by parachute. He was immediately attacked by civilians and received fatal injuries.
6. Junction Buckingham Palace Rd and Ebury Bridge Rd, where the Hurricane crashed.
7. Block of flats in Ebury Bridge Road where Ray Holmes landed by parachute.
8. Harleyford Road, Ron McGill.
9. Victoria Coach Station, Reg Garman.
10. Newburn Street, Kathleen Hatton.

block of flats. At first the pilot thought he would pass close over the top of the building, but he slammed into the roof and his parachute immediately collapsed, leaving him with no visible means of support. 'I tried to grab something to halt my fall but it was no good, I slithered down the tiles. Everybody knows you can't fall off the roof of a three-storey building and get away with it. As I slithered past the gutter I thought, "This is it. After all I've been through, I'm going to break my neck falling off a roof . . ."'

Yet even now the pilot's run of luck held. The ground was coming up to meet him, fast, then: 'There was a terrible jolt . . . and I came to a stop just off the ground! The canopy had caught over an up-spout! I came to rest, my toes just touching the bottom of an empty dust-bin with the lid off.'

Next to reach the ground were the lighter items that had broken from the Dornier. The severed tail came down on the roof of a house in Vauxhall Bridge Road. The bomber's wings, borne by the north-easterly wind, fluttered on for more than a mile before they finally came to earth south of the Thames. Seventeen-year-old embroidress Kathleen Hatton, at her parents' flat at Newburn Street, Vauxhall, heard a noise outside and went on to the balcony to see what was happening. One of the wing sections just missed her. 'It passed inches in front of my face, then went clatter . . . clatter . . . clatter as it bounced against the side of the building before ending up on the ground.' Shaken by the narrow escape, she drew back into the building.

IN AN AIR BATTLE events follow each other with great rapidity. Everything described in this narrative, from the start of the Dorniers' bombing run until the wing of one of them clattered to the ground in Vauxhall, took place in just five minutes: between 12.10 and 12.15 on that fateful Sunday afternoon.

SOUTH-EAST LONDON, 12.16 P.M. With both engines shot out, Rolf Heitsch's main concern was to get the bomber to the ground in one piece. So long as he retained a measure of control there could be no question of bailing out and leaving the semi-conscious radio operator to his fate. Sensing that the bomber was finished, the fighter pilots circled their victim and followed it down. Heitsch made a wheels-up landing in a meadow just north of Sevenoaks, narrowly missing several cows grazing there. The second Dornier had gone down.

The third Dornier to go down was Wilhelm Raab's aircraft, described in the Prologue. This bomber crashed south of Sevenoaks, about five miles from where Heitsch landed.

ANOTHER OF THE Dorniers was forced out of the formation of Pilot Officer Jim Meaker of No. 249 Squadron. The bomber's port engine came to a stop and as the plane dived away the Hurricane pilot attacked again, now concentrating on the starboard engine. In his diary Meaker described the action in graphic detail:

> Follow him, plugging all the time. A quarter attack comes off beautifully, see bullets going in, in a line from the nose back to the tail, at intervals of a foot all the way down. See that the rear gunner is lying back in his seat, probably dead. Dornier is smoking like a chimney, can smell it from behind him, oil comes back on my aircraft and pieces fly past me. Then three blasted Spitfires horn in and drive me away from my own private and personal Dornier.

Oberleutnant Karl-Ernst Wilke, navigator in Meaker's 'private and personal Dornier', described the mayhem caused by the attacks. 'Unteroffizier Schatz was the first to be killed. His task was to operate the guns on each side of the cabin, to provide defence against attacks from the left or the right. The poor guy was hit during the initial attack,' Wilke later wrote. 'Then I was hit by a bullet from the right, it struck my face just below the nose and blinded me. From that moment I took no further part in the action.' A fire broke out in the cabin and the radio operator suffered severe burns. The Dornier was in a hopeless position and the pilot ordered the survivors to bail out. The radio operator crawled to the escape hatch, released it and jumped. Wilke followed.

The three Spitfires that had 'horned in' on the Dornier were flown by Flight Lieutenant Gillies and Pilot Officer Bodie of No. 66 Squadron, and Pilot Officer Pollard of No. 611 Squadron. All three pilots fired long bursts into the crippled bomber, and observed the two crewmen jump clear. Then Bodie went in for a closer look at the bomber:

> He was pretty well riddled. Eight machine-guns certainly make a mess. I had a look at the pilot. He sat bolt upright in his seat and was either dead or wounded for he didn't turn his head to look at me or watch out for a place to land, but stared straight ahead . . .
> The machine went on. The pilot was dead. He made no attempt

to flatten out and land, but went smack into a field and the aeroplane exploded. I saw the pieces sail past me as I flew low overhead. I didn't feel particularly jubilant.

The plane crashed about four miles east of Canterbury. The fourth Dornier had gone down.

YET ANOTHER of the Dorniers was forced out of formation, and tried to escape by heading south. Four Hurricane pilots went after it: Sergeant Hurry of No. 46 squadron, Pilot Officer Ortmans and Sergeant O'Manney of No. 229 Squadron and Pilot Officer White of No. 504 Squadron. The fighters hounded the bomber all the way to the ground, taking turns to attack the enemy plane as it weaved in and out of the trees, trying desperately to shake them off.

George Tuke, a fourteen-year-old cycling near his home at Mayfield, witnessed the bomber's final moments. 'Suddenly I heard the roar of aircraft engines and the sound of machine-gun fire' he later recounted. 'It started to get unhealthy where I was – I was in the overshoot of the bullets! I half fell, half jumped off my bike and scrambled behind a hedge. I peeped up, and saw a Dornier being attacked by three Hurricanes. There was no let-up in the attacks, the planes were going round in a circle. Bits fell off the Dornier, its port engine was on fire.'

Then the schoolboy saw a flash above the Dornier: the sun glinting off the top escape hatch as it fell away. A crew member immediately followed but he pulled his ripcord a split second too soon. The opening parachute caught on the tail of the bomber, leaving the unfortunate man trailing behind. With the partially open parachute canopy acting as a giant air-brake, the bomber stalled and fell out of the sky. The plane plunged into the small wood and the fuel tanks exploded with a *wooomph*. A cloud of oily black smoke rose to mark the crash site. There were no survivors from the fifth Dornier to go down.

The sixth Dornier lost also tried to get home alone, flying over the Thames Estuary. Pilot Officer Tony Barton of No. 253 Squadron caught up with it and ran in to attack: 'I delivered three head-on attacks, firing for about three seconds in each attack. He turned and made off south, losing height after the second attack. After the third attack he appeared to have lost control to a certain extent: he circled and lost height. About eight minutes after my having ceased fire he crashed in the sea about four miles north-west of Herne Bay.' Again there were no survivors.

Near Maidstone, the Messerschmitt 109s assigned to cover the Dorniers' withdrawal linked up with the main formation and shepherded the survivors home. Assisting the bombers on the way out was the same 90 m.p.h. wind that had impeded them on the way in.

Of the twenty-five bombers that had crossed the coast of England three-quarters of an hour earlier, only fifteen remained in formation and most of those were damaged. As we have seen, six had been shot down. The remaining four Dorniers were struggling home alone. By judicious use of cloud, and a measure of luck, all would reach France.

Bomber Geschwader 76 had taken a fearful mauling. But, given the lack of escorts and the overwhelming concentration of fighters engaging the formation over London, it is surprising that any Dornier survived. That three-quarters of the German force did so is testimony of the leadership of Major Alois Lindmayr, and the discipline and flying skill of his crews. Despite the intensive attacks by RAF fighters, the majority of the bomber crews held their place in formation and traded blows with their assailants. The formation was still intact when its 'Seventh Cavalry', the Messerschmitts of the withdrawal covering force, linked up with it. By any yardstick Lindmayr had conducted a remarkably successful fighting withdrawal.

AS WELL AS the main action around the bombers, there were several venomous little confrontations between the opposing fighters. Sergeant David Cox of No. 19 Squadron was separated from his unit during a tussle with Messerschmitts, and headed south. 'We were told that if we became separated from our squadron we should join up with any friendly aircraft in the area,' he later recalled. 'After a few minutes I saw six aircraft out to my right. They were flying north, in the opposite direction to me, not very far off. They looked like Hurricanes so I turned towards them. And then I realized they were Me 109s . . .'

The nearest two pairs went underneath the Spitfire and that was the last he saw of them. 'The remaining two climbed, one went behind me and the other went in front. Naturally, it was the one behind me I was the more interested in. I turned into him and got inside him. Then he bunted and dived away.' Cox did a quarter-turn and saw the other Messerschmitt about 600 yards away and a little above, about to fly across his nose. 'I aimed well in front and opened fire. His aircraft flew right through my rounds, he disappeared into the smoke of my tracers then turned slowly to port, his nose dropped and he started to go down through cloud.' Possibly the Messerschmitt Cox hit was that which forced-landed soon afterwards near Uckfield, with damage to the engine cooling system. The pilot, unhurt, was taken prisoner.

Sergeant 'Ginger' Lacey of No. 501 Squadron was also separated from his unit and, like Cox, he headed to join up with some fighters he saw in the distance. And, like Cox, he found they were Messerschmitts. When the truth dawned, Lacey's Hurricane was closing head-on with about a dozen of the enemy. Instinctively he pushed his stick forward to build up speed and get into the blind zone below the German fighters. The Messerschmitts swept overhead and he waited for them to turn and come after him. But they continued straight ahead. They had not seen him! Sensing an opportunity too good to miss, Lacey hauled the Hurricane into a loop that brought him into a firing position inverted but 150 yards behind the rear Messerschmitt. Lacey fired a short burst and, trailing smoke, the Messerschmitt dived away.

Lacey rolled his fighter right-way-up and waited to see what the other Messerschmitts would do. To his surprise they continued straight on: still they had not noticed anything! The range had opened to about 250 yards but he was still in a firing position. He placed his sight over another of the Messerschmitts and opened fire again; a second German fighter fell away from the formation trailing smoke. At last aware of the presence of their lone assailant, the Messerschmitts suddenly split into two groups and swung round after the Hurricane. Lacey peeled into a steep dive heading for cloud, hoping the Messerschmitts did not have the fuel for a long chase. The Hurricane plunged into the cloud and Lacey emerged out of the bottom, before easing on the stick to pull out. A careful search to the rear revealed no enemy fighters: the Messerschmitts had not followed. Lacey had carried out a daring, some might say foolhardy, attack on a dozen enemy fighters and got away with it.

Staying low and maintaining a continual scan of the sky around, he set course for Kenley.

KENNINGTON, 12.25 P.M. Of the three German crewmen who parachuted from the Dornier that crashed beside Victoria station, before Ray Holmes rammed it, two were taken into captivity almost immediately after they reached the ground. The pilot, Oberleutnant Robert Zehbe, was less fortunate. He came down in Kennington, a part of London which had suffered in earlier raids and whose citizens were in no mood to observe the courtesies of war. As Ron McGill's mother tugged at his collar to get him home, the boy saw knots of angry men and women hastening along Harleyford Road towards the point where the descending parachute was expected to land.

Waiting for their bus to resume its journey, Walter Chesney and his wife had been sheltering in an archway opposite the Oval underground station. Suddenly the German airman appeared beside them a few yards away, as if from nowhere. 'His parachute caught over electric power cables and he ended up dangling just above the ground. People came from all directions shouting "Kill him, kill him!" They pulled him down, they went crazy. Some women arrived carrying knives and pokers and they went straight in and attacked him,' Chesney remembered. 'In the end an army truck arrived and the half-dozen soldiers had to fight their way through the crowd to get to him. They put him in the back of the truck and drove off.' Fatally wounded by the mob, the airman died soon afterwards.

CHELSEA, 12.25 P.M. Seventy-five exciting minutes after he had left his bath, Ray Holmes was back on the ground. Still in one piece after nearly crashing into one Dornier, ramming another, escaping from his Hurricane and falling off the roof of the block of flats, the young pilot had considerable grounds for elation. As he undid his parachute harness and stepped from the dustbin where the parachute had deposited him, he shouted 'Is there anybody around?' Two girls appeared in the garden of the next flat and the pilot, overjoyed at still being alive, jumped the fence and kissed both!

Shortly afterwards a Home Guardsman arrived to assist the pilot, and willingly agreed to take him to the point about 400 yards away where the Hurricane had crashed. 'There were a lot of people in the street. I thought I might steal a look at my aircraft without being noticed, but when the people realized who I was I got enthusiastic slaps on the back. That did my shoulder no good at all, it was very painful if anyone touched it,' Holmes later commented. 'Where the Hurricane had gone in, there was a hole like a bomb crater about fifteen feet deep. The aircraft must have gone down almost vertically. It was in the middle of a crossroads with tall buildings and blocks of flats all around, but apart from the odd broken window none of the buildings was damaged.'

The injured pilot was taken to Chelsea Barracks where an Army doctor examined the shoulder. Apart from splintering one of the bones there was nothing seriously wrong. Holmes was then escorted to the Officers' Mess for drinks to celebrate his aerial victory and subsequent survival. While there an army major edged up to the pilot and asked quietly: 'Excuse me, old boy, but do you always fly dressed like that?' Holmes glanced down and realized how odd he must have looked. Having lost his flying boots when he bailed out, he now stood in his socks; he wore service trousers, the blue sports shirt he had pulled on when he jumped from his bath, and a yellow life jacket.

After a few drinks a taxi was ordered and, compliments of the Army, Holmes returned to Hendon in style.

CHELSEA, 12.54 P.M. The all-clear sounded and Jack Hill was released from duty as an air-raid warden. He decided to walk to Victoria station to see the wrecked German plane. The main part of the Dornier had crashed on the station forecourt, immediately beside a jeweller's shop. Like the Hurricane nearby, the bomber had fallen on a built-up area but it caused remarkably little damage and no casualties on the ground. When Hill arrived a large crowd had assembled, but a police cordon prevented those without official business from approaching the wreckage.

AFTER BELLY-LANDING his Dornier north of Sevenoaks, Rolf Heitsch and his crew had a struggle to open the escape hatch above the cabin. When it was off they carefully lifted the unconscious radio operator from the bomber and laid him on the grass. The man was bleeding profusely from chest wounds. Before the war Heitsch had trained as a doctor, and could see that his crewman was beyond medical care. Shortly afterwards seven or eight Home Guardsmen arrived on the scene, some armed with shotguns. A car arrived to collect the wounded man and take him to hospital, but he died soon after arrival. Heitsch and the other crewmen were marched over fields to a lorry waiting to take them into captivity.

SOUTH OF TUNBRIDGE WELLS, George Tuke made his way to the remains of the Dornier he had watched crash, following the frenzied low-altitude chase by Hurricanes. Although some parts were still on fire and rounds of ammunition exploded from time to time, such hazards were insufficient to deter a schoolboy bent on adding to his collection of war mementoes. 'There were bits of wreckage littered around. The parachute was still draped over the tail and the body of the crewman was caught up in the branches of an oak tree.' Tuke found a small suitcase on the ground, in almost perfect condition. 'It was an overnight bag belonging to one of the crew. It contained a shaving kit and personal belongings, including a pair of black leather dancing pumps. Why he had brought them to England I cannot imagine, but they were there.'

12:10 P.M., BATTERSEA. The exploding bombs had cut the railway tracks passing through Battersea in several places. Part of the Pouparts Viaduct had fallen on the track below, and the presence of four unexploded bombs delayed repairs. All rail traffic through the area was halted.

In the residential areas along each side of the tracks, civil defence workers strove to rescue the living, remove the dead and wounded and restore a semblance of order. Reports of damage and casualties streamed into the Battersea civil defence headquarters; a few of these, reproduced below, convey an idea of the calamity that had befallen the community.

> Two women who have been suffering from shock are now ready to go home, but they have no homes to go to. Where shall they go, and could a car take them as they are not yet fit to go alone?

> Elesley Road. HE [high explosive] bombs. Damage to water and gas mains. Elesley Road from Tyneham Road to Graysham Road blocked. Nos 12, 14, 18, 20, 27, 29, 31, 33, 35, 37, in danger of collapse. Gideon Road School damaged.

Beaufoy Road. HE bomb. Road blocked from Hanbury Road to Lavender Hill. Nos 69, 71, 73 Beaufoy Road demolished, adjoining houses in danger of collapse.

Water running through gas pipe Tritton Street and surrounding streets.

Kersley Street. HE bomb. Damage to water, gas, electricity mains and sewers. Nos 24, 26, 28 at junction Battersea Bridge Road demolished. 2 people with shock.

Sabine Road. HE bomb. Sabine Road blocked from Tyneham Road to Grayshot Road, Nos 26, 28, 30, 32, 42, and 44 in danger of collapse.

Tyneham Road, junction of Ashbury Road. HE bomb. Large crater in middle of road.

In the boroughs of Battersea and Clapham twenty-four people had been killed and more than thirty injured. The worst incident was at Kenwyn Road, Clapham, where five people were killed when their home was hit.

Immediately after the raid, Police Constable Bernard Tucker's first duty was to go to Nine Elms gas works and check that the policeman guarding the plant was unhurt. As he approached, Tucker was careful to identify himself; his colleague had a loaded revolver and had orders to use it if anyone attempted to sabotage the installation. The other man had also heard the descent of the bomb that had not exploded, but was not permitted to leave his post at the entrance to the works. Now Tucker went to the spot where his comrade thought the bomb had come down: 'I arrived to see a slight disturbance of the ground where the bomb had entered the soil. Earth had fallen back and covered the entry hole.' He hastened back to the police station to report the find. Later that day, army engineers would render the bomb safe and remove it.

After the bombs ceased exploding, Winifred Kingman walked through the opening where her front door had been. Standing in Shellwood Road, she saw that the cause of the damage was a bomb that had landed on the house opposite, demolishing it. Her neighbours, she later learned, had been away at the time visiting friends. Then she turned to inspect her own home. Except for a few broken windows the sole damage was to the front door which, by a quirk of the blast, had been sucked away from the house. It was as if a giant hand had wrenched the door off its hinges and laid it gently on the garden path.

When his shift ended Bernard Tucker left the police station and cycled home. In Tyneham Road he had to skirt round a bomb crater in the middle of the road. 'There was very little damage, just a few windows smashed and leaves blown off trees. The telephone lines had been blown down, they were lying all over the place. An old man stood guard over the wires and shouted at me, "Don't touch those, you'll get a shock!" I was able to assure him there was no risk of a shock from telephone wires, and he calmed down.'

BY 12:45 P.M. the last of the raiders had left England, and the all-clear sounded in the capital. During the action the Royal Air Force fighter controllers had turned in an exemplary perform-ance: twenty-three squadrons of Spitfires and Hurricanes had been scrambled, and all except one had engaged the enemy.

During the return flight over the English Channel, Fighter Geschwader 3 lost a Messerschmitt 109 in unusual circum-stances. Feldwebel Volmer was descending towards Calais when his fighter suddenly flipped on its back and fell into a vertical dive. No British aircraft were in the vicinity, and Germans in the area saw no sign of hostile action. Despite radio warnings to the pilot to bail out, he remained in the cockpit until the aircraft plunged into the sea. A subsequent investigation failed to establish the cause of the loss.

The German escort force lost nine Messerschmitts destroyed and two more damaged. For its part, Fighter Command had lost two Spitfires and eleven Hurricanes destroyed, and two Spitfires and nine Hurricanes damaged. More important, the action had demonstrated that Air Chief Marshal Dowding's fighters were far from beaten.

As the raiders left the coast, a calm of sorts returned to south-east England. Now we shift our attention to other events on that momentous day.

Chapter 3

INTERLUDE

1.00 to 1.45 p.m.

The object of a good general is not to fight, but to win. He has fought enough if he gains a victory.

The Duke of Alba

UXBRIDGE, 1.00 P.M. On the plotting table at No. 11 Group headquarters, the markers representing German formations inched their way across the English Channel and back to France. Then, one by one, the markers came off the board as plots ceased when the planes descended below the radar horizon.

In the operations room the morning shift had remained on duty well beyond the scheduled relief time. It was 'not done' to change shifts during an action; that would have disrupted the flow of the plotting. Before the plotting team was stood down, there were felicitations from a beaming Prime Minister. 'After the action Winston Churchill came down to the floor of the operations room to congratulate us on our work,' Vera Saies recalled. 'He looked round the operations room and said "Well done!" in that deep voice of his.'

NORTH WEALD, 1.05 P.M. In a scene repeated at airfields all over the south of England, the Spitfires and Hurricanes streamed back to their bases in ones and twos and landed. As each taxied into its dispersal area, the pilot shut down his engine and climbed out of the cockpit. Ground crewmen gathered round to learn how he had done, how well the fighter had performed and what, if anything, required attention. The tasks of refuelling and rearming the fighters began immediately, to return the machines to battle-readiness as soon as possible.

Pilot Officer Tom Neil of No. 249 Squadron wrote of his return to North Weald:

> My crew were excited when I returned, the charred gun ports a sure sign of action. Running towards me, their enthusiasm waned when my face told the story. Nothing? Hard luck, sir, they sympathized.
>
> They hooked up the bowser and tore off the wing panels to rearm the guns with endless yards of bullets. Guns OK? I thought so; they didn't stop, anyway. A man dragging oxygen in my direction. Engine all right, sir? I said that it was but thought fit to complain of oil from the airscrew. Couldn't see to hit anything if the windscreen was covered with goo, could I? They agreed and set about cleaning it and inspecting the front where yellow smears feet long trailed back along the front cowlings. Also for bullet holes. Had I been hit? I didn't think so, but you never could tell. They searched – hopefully.

Leaving their planes in the capable hands of the ground crews, the pilots sauntered to the squadron dispersal hut where the intelligence officer waited to question each. Anyone claiming an enemy plane destroyed or damaged had to write a combat report giving the details. During the noon action No. 249 Squadron claimed one Dornier destroyed, another probably destroyed and an Me 109 damaged for no loss to itself. Tom Neil continued:

> A lot of chatter. A few Huns being claimed as 'probable' or 'damaged' by unidentified voices. Not a great squadron success, though. Odd that, because it should have been.
>
> Lunch arrived with combat reports, plates and food sharing the same table. I sat on my bed, eating. Not too happy with life. Finally, I lay back and, still in my Mae West, slept. Like a log.

PAS DE CALAIS, 1.05 P.M. Of the Dorniers of Bomber Geschwader 76 that regained the coast of France, the first to put down was Oberleutnant Benno Hermann's. Badly shot up, the bomber made a belly landing near Boulogne with one crewman dead and two wounded. The plane was damaged beyond repair.

Unteroffizier Hans Figge, his Dornier hit by more than two hundred rounds and flying on one engine, got as far as Poix before the other engine gave out and he made a crash landing. This bomber, too, was damaged beyond repair.

Shortly after 2 p.m. the rest of the Dorniers began landing at their bases at Beauvais and Cormeilles-en-Vexin. Almost all bore the scars of battle. Feldwebel Kurt Uhlman's had more than seventy hits. Unteroffizier Hanke's aircraft, in which Theodor

Rehm was navigator, returned with forty-seven hits and shot-out tyres on the left main wheel and the tail wheel.

ST PAUL'S CATHEDRAL, LONDON. As the noon attack ended, the three-day operation to remove the 2,200-pound bomb beneath St Paul's cathedral entered its final phase. During the late morning Army engineers had reached the bomb and Lieutenant Davies descended the shaft and inspected the weapon. Sappers then ran a thick rope through the block suspended from sheerlegs above the hole. One end was secured to the bomb, the other to the towing hook of a lorry. A second lorry backed into position in front of the first and was linked to it by a tow rope. Now the extraction operation could begin.

With a revving of engines in low gear the lorries edged forwards and the mud-caked bomb, nine feet long, rose slowly up the shaft like a huge malignant molar. When the bomb was well clear of the ground the front lorry was unhitched and driven up to the shaft, then the bomb was carefully lowered on to the bed of the vehicle and roped down. Davies climbed into the driver's cab and started on the five-mile drive to the 'bomb cemetery' on Hackney Marshes.

By the time the vehicle reached Hackney, police loud-speaker cars had toured the borough giving warning of the impending detonation of another German bomb on the nearby marshes. Residents were enjoined to open all windows, to reduce the risk of the panes being shattered by blast.

The 2,200-pounder went off with a bang heard several miles away. Living in a block of flats overlooking the marshes, Mrs Lily Hudson later told a press reporter, 'We postponed Sunday dinner for the explosion. Although we were prepared for it, it was rather stunning when it came.'

ALSO AT around mid-day Royal Air Force Bomber Command dispatched six Blenheims to carry out individual nuisance raids on Calais, Ostend, Dunkirk, Antwerp, Zeebrugge and Flushing. In each case there was insufficient cloud cover to allow the attack to proceed and, in accordance with orders, the missions were abandoned. In a separate operation, six more Blenheims flew an armed reconnaissance sweep over the North Sea. There was no contact with the enemy and all the bombers returned safely.

ON THAT DAY Royal Air Force Coastal Command aircraft flew a total of ninety-five sorties which included anti-invasion and anti-submarine patrols, minelaying and photographic reconnaissance missions.

Of particular interest to this account were the operations by the Spitfires of the Photographic Reconnaissance Unit, a squadron-sized unit charged with keeping a day-to-day watch on the German invasion preparations. Carrying cameras and extra fuel tanks instead of guns and relying on speed and altitude to avoid interception, on that day the Spitfires photographed every major port between Antwerp and Cherbourg.

The latest batch of aerial photographs revealed significant new developments. At Antwerp there were 6 more merchant ships tied up at the quayside, bringing the total there to 16. At Zeebrugge the number was the same as before: 7 large merchant ships, 15 tugs and 30 barges. At Flushing no change, 150 barges. A large passenger ship escorted by 4 torpedo-boats was photographed off Calais. At Boulogne there were 30 barges more than on the previous reconnaissance, bringing the total there to 120, in addition to 150 other small craft. Approaching Le Treport was an armada of 35 small boats. At Cherbourg there was no change: 5 destroyers, 6 torpedo-boats, 9 minesweepers, 4 fast patrol-boats and 15 merchant vessels. The reconnaissance photographs provided evidence aplenty that the invasion preparations were at an advanced stage.

All Coastal Command's aircraft returned safely from the day's operations.

Chapter 4

THE MID-AFTERNOON ATTACK ON LONDON

1.45 p.m. to 3.45 p.m.

It is in the use and withholding of their reserves that the great commanders have generally excelled. After all, when once the last reserve has been thrown in, the commander's part is played . . . The event must be left to the pluck of the fighting troops.

Winston Churchill

EVEN BEFORE the last of the noon raiders had left the coast of England, the German bombers assigned to the next attack were already airborne, assembled in formation and climbing towards the Pas de Calais. First to take off had been the Heinkels of Bomber Geschwader 53, based at airfields around Lille in northeast France. Next were the Dorniers of Bomber Geschwader 2, from St Leger and Cambrai. Then came the Heinkels of Bomber Geschwader 26 from Wevelghem and Gilze Rijen, and finally more Dorniers from Bomber Geschwader 3 based at Antwerp in Belgium. The bombers' targets were the docks and warehouses in the East End of London: the Royal Victoria and the West India Docks to the north of the Thames, and the Surrey Commercial Docks to the south.

Those in the German planes viewed the forthcoming attack with mixed feelings. Holding formation with other Dorniers of Bomber Geschwader 3, Feldwebel Horst Schulz was on his first combat mission and was excited at the prospect of attacking London. Leutnant Roderich Cescotti, at the controls of a Heinkel of Bomber Geschwader 26, was less sanguine; this was his sixteenth war sortie and he had lost several good friends during previous attacks on England. From below the bombers, scores of Messerschmitt 109s came spiralling up to rendezvous with their assigned bomber formations. Piloting one of them was Ober-leutnant Hans Schmoller-Haldy of Fighter Geschwader 54, lead-ing a four-aircraft Schwarm providing close escort for Cescotti's formation. Schmoller-Haldy had the usual butterflies in his stomach at the start of a mission; always there was the worry of having to re-cross the stretch of water to get home after the action, perhaps in a damaged fighter.

UXBRIDGE, 1.45 P.M. As the leading German aircraft came into view of the British coastal radars, a rash of 'hostile' plots appeared on the No. 11 Group plotting table. This time the fighter controller's first reaction was to order a single Spitfire to scramble from Hawkinge. Hawkinge near Folkestone was the furthest forward and therefore the most exposed of Fighter Command's airfields, being less than thirty miles from the German assembly area. The Spitfire's pilot, Flying Officer Alan Wright of No. 92 Squadron, had flown in from his base at Biggin Hill during the late morning and waited in his cockpit until the next raiding force was detected. Now, having received the scramble order, he was to fly a 'Spotter' mission: to get as high as possible over mid-Channel and report on the strength and composition of the incoming German force.

Over the next ten minutes Air Vice-Marshal Park and the Prime Minister watched the build-up of the enemy forces over the Pas de Calais. The radar operators assessed the strengths of the three largest enemy formations at 50-plus, 60-plus and 30-plus, and the total strength of the five smaller ones at 85-plus. In contrast to that during the morning action, this 'guestimate' was wide of the mark. The force assembling comprised some 475 aircraft, making the radar operators' assessment of 225-plus aircraft an underestimate by about half.

Shortly before 2 p.m., before the vanguard of the raiders left the French coast, Park started to deploy his fighters. The pro-cedure was similar to that of a couple of hours earlier, with four pairs of squadrons ordered to scramble and move to patrol over Sheerness, Chelmsford, Hornchurch and Kenley.

NORTH WEALD, 2 P.M. Fast asleep on his bed in the hut at No. 249 Squadron's dispersal area, Tom Neil had a rude awakening.

Fighter Command Initial Wave of Scrambles, 2.00 p.m.

Time	Sector	Disposition
Airborne		
No. 11 Group		
2.00	Hornchurch	Nos 222 and 603 Squadrons, 20 Spitfires, to Sheerness at 20,000 feet (failed to join up; squadrons would go into action singly).
	Debden	Nos 17 and 257 Squadrons, 20 Hurricanes, to Chelmsford at 15,000 feet.
	Kenley	Nos 501 and 605 Squadrons, 17 Hurricanes, to Kenley at 5,000 feet.
	North Weald	Nos 249 and 504 Squadrons, 21 Hurricanes, to Hornchurch at 15,000 feet.

'I was dragged from the deepest pit of unconsciousness by the telephone and the bellowed cry of "Scramble". Rolling off my bed, I followed in the wake of the thumping boots like a zombie. Two o'clock, for God's sake! What were the Huns doing to us?' Neil stumbled to his Hurricane, climbed into the cockpit, started the engine and followed the rest of the planes to the down-wind end of the airfield. In ones and twos the fighters turned into wind and began taking off.

NORTH OF BOULOGNE, 2.05 P.M. Their escorts in place, the phalanx of German bombers set course for Dungeness. At the head of the force were 43 Dorniers of Bomber Geschwader 2; next, a couple of miles behind, came 24 Heinkels of Bomber Geschwader 53; finally, a couple of miles further behind, came 19 Dorniers of Bomber Geschwader 3 followed by 28 Heinkels of Bomber Geschwader 26. The attacking force of 114 bombers advanced towards Kent at an air speed of 180 m.p.h., passing 14,000 feet in a slow climb and, as during the previous attack, battling against the same north-westerly headwind.

Hans Schmoller-Haldy detested close-escort missions. His orders were to remain close to the bombers until forced to break away by shortage of fuel. If he left his charges for any other reason he knew there would be recriminations when he got back. 'Our mission was to provide close escort, which I loathed. It gave the bomber crews the feeling they were being protected, and it might have deterred some of the enemy pilots. But for us fighter pilots it was very bad. We needed the advantages of altitude and speed so we could engage the enemy on favourable terms. As it was, the British fighters had the initiative of when and how to attack.' The Messerschmitts flew at 230 m.p.h., weaving from side to side to keep station on the bombers cruising at 180 m.p.h. 'We needed to maintain speed, otherwise the Me 109s would have taken too long to accelerate to fighting speed if we were bounced by Spitfires,' Schmoller-Haldy explained.

Ahead, partly covered by cloud, Schmoller-Haldy could make out the now-familiar cliffs of Kent. The sight evoked memories of Shakespeare's soliloquy on England from *Richard II*, that he had learned in translation at school:

This other Eden, demi-paradise,
This earth of majesty, this seat of Mars,
This fortress built by Nature for herself
Against infection and the hand of war . . .

The German pilot forced these musings from his mind. He knew that if he failed to keep his wits about him, he could expect no quarter from the defenders of that sceptred isle.

TWENTY-SIX THOUSAND FEET OVER THE STRAIT OF DOVER, 2.05 P.M. High up and feeling very alone, Alan Wright squinted from his Spitfire for signs of the approaching enemy. Far below, over mid-Channel, he could make out a cluster of black specks too far away to identify. He reported these by radio and was moving in for a closer look, when he noticed six Messerschmitts climbing towards him. 'When they got to about 2,000 feet below me, I thought the time had come to take the initiative. I went down to attack and the Messerschmitt I was after turned north and went into a steep dive. I took a shot from about 500 yards, and to my surprise he steepened his dive. I started to catch up and fired another burst from 250 yards. He was diving at about 70 degrees, it was as much as I could do to keep after him.'

In the dive the Spitfire rapidly built up speed. Wright had omitted to re-trim the plane at the start of the dive, and now he had to push hard on the stick with both hands to hold the fighter's nose down. He had no spare hand to re-trim the fighter and so reduce the stick forces. At such speeds the Spitfire's ailerons were almost immovable, and try as he might he was unable to get his gunsight back on the Messerschmitt. Wright decided to abandon the pursuit and for an instant he relaxed his forward pressure on the stick. The next thing he knew the Spitfire had asserted its will and was pulling itself out of the dive. 'It pulled out so sharply, the G forces were so strong, that I passed out. I have no idea what happened next. When I came to it was like coming out of an anaesthetic. The Spitfire was upside down at about 7,000 feet, flying at 150 m.p.h. It took me some time to pull myself together, to recall that I had been in a combat and what had happened.' Wright rolled the fighter right way up, and, with a numbing realization of his vulnerability to attack from the enemy planes in the area, he turned north and sped out of the area as fast as the Spitfire would carry him. He made himself a strict rule that the next time he entered a steep dive in combat, he would first re-trim his fighter . . .

UXBRIDGE, 2.05 P.M. While Alan Wright was regaining his composure after the harrowing experience, Air Vice-Marshal Park scrambled four more fighter squadrons. By now the plotting table showed three separate enemy forces heading for Dungeness: the three columns of bombers and the fighters of the close-escort forces. More spread out, coming in faster and moving towards the coast between Dungeness and Dover, were five more concentrations of enemy planes: fighters on free-hunting patrols taking the direct route to London.

A few minutes later Park ordered off a further eight squadrons. He also told his senior controller, Willoughby de Broke, to request Nos 10 and 12 Groups to send their squadrons to defend the capital too.

Fighter Command's Second Wave of Scrambles, 2.05 to 2.15 p.m.

Time	Sector	Disposition
Airborne No. 11 Group		
2.05	Biggin Hill	Nos 41 and 92 Squadrons, 20 Spitfires, to Hornchurch at 20,000 feet.
	Northolt	Nos 1 (Canadian) and 229 Squadrons, 21 Hurricanes, to Northolt.
2.10	North Weald	No. 46 Squadron, 9 Hurricanes, to London docks.
	Biggin Hill	Nos 66 and 72 Squadrons, 20 Spitfires, to Biggin Hill at 20,000 feet.

	Debden Sector	No. 73 Squadron, 6 Hurricanes, to Maidstone at 15,000 feet.
2.15	Kenley	No. 253 Squadron, 9 Hurricanes, to Kenley at 15,000 feet.
	Tangmere	Nos 213 and 607 Squadrons, 23 Hurricanes, to Kenley–Biggin Hill area at 15,000 feet.

No. 10 Group

2.15	Middle Wallop	No. 238 Squadron, 12 Hurricanes, to Kenley area.

No. 12 Group

2.15	Duxford	Big Wing, Nos 19, 242, 302, 310 and 311 Squadrons, 20 Spitfires and 27 Hurricanes, to Hornchurch at 25,000 feet.

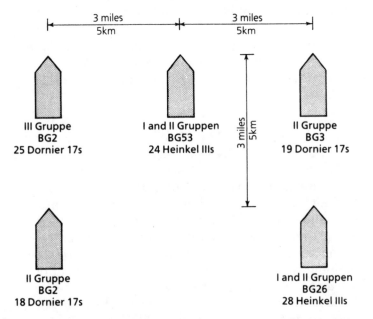

The German Attack Force at 2.10 p.m., in battle order after crossing the coast at Dungeness.

Each of the Bomber formations had one Gruppe (about 30) Me 109s flying as close escort. Five more Gruppen of fighters flew extended cover round the force as a whole, and a further five Gruppen of fighters flew in the free-hunting role ahead and on the flanks of the force.

77

DUNGENESS, 2.10 P.M. As the vanguard of the German bomber force passed over the distinctive promontory on the south coast of Kent, all three forces of bombers wheeled sedately until they were heading north-north-west. The move put the raiders into their planned attack formation with the three forces of bombers in line abreast about three miles apart: on the left the Dorniers of Bomber Geschwader 2, in the middle the Heinkels of Bomber Geschwader 53 and on the right the Dorniers of Bomber Geschwader 3 followed by the Heinkels of Bomber Geschwader 26. Feldwebel Heinz Kirsch of Bomber Geschwader 3 described the mood in his Dornier as it crossed the coast: 'In our aircraft there was complete calm. The radio was silent. The safety catches were off, our steel helmets were on and each man searched his individual sector. Of the enemy there was nothing to be seen. In recent actions we had not had much contact with British fighters. We felt safe protected by the ME 109s.'

Since the noon attack the cloud over south-east England had thickened a little and increased in vertical extent. Now there was seven-tenths cumulus, base at 3,000 feet and tops extending in places to 12,000 feet.

WEST HAM, LONDON, 2.12 P.M. When she was not working as a railway booking clerk, 24-year-old Irene Cannon was part of the civil defence organization. Wearing her dark blue Air-Raid Precautions uniform, she and her husband were at home finishing their Sunday lunch. There was an urgent knock on the front door and she was told to go to her post immediately: Air-Raid Warning Yellow was in force and the civil defence organization was being brought to readiness. She grabbed the bag containing her steel helmet and gas mask and set out at a brisk pace for Star Lane School fifty yards away, requisitioned as an ARP post and reception centre. As she reached the building, the sirens sounded to announce Air-Raid Warning Red – attack imminent.

ABOVE ROMNEY MARSH, 2.15 P.M. Again Air Vice-Marshal Park's forward-deployed Spitfire squadrons went into action soon after the raiders crossed the coast. The initial clash involved Nos 41, 92 and 222 Squadrons, with twenty-seven fighters, and

The Route of the German Attack Force to London.

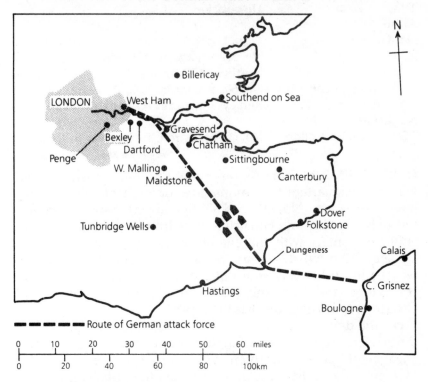

Route of German attack force

these immediately became entangled with the escorting Messerschmitts.

One German pilot involved in the action was Hauptmann Fritz Losigkeit of Fighter Geschwader 26: 'After we crossed the coast the British fighters came in from a great height, going very fast,' he recalled. 'They broke through to the He 111s ahead of us and below, to attack the rear of the formation. During the dive some of the Spitfires became detached from the others. Using full throttle, my Staffel was able to catch up with them and I got into an attacking position. I fired a long burst and pieces broke away from the Spitfire's wing and fuselage. The pilot slid back the canopy and jumped from the cockpit. Overtaking rapidly, I pulled to the left of the Spitfire and saw his parachute open.'

The pilot of the Spitfire was probably Pilot Officer Bob Holland of No. 92 Squadron, who was forced to bail out at about this time and suffered minor injuires on landing.

Fighter Command's Third Wave of Scrambles, 2.20 to 2.30 p.m.

Time Airborne	Sector	Disposition
No. 11 Group		
2.20	Northolt	No. 303 Squadron, 9 Hurricanes, to Northolt at 20,000 feet.
	Tangmere	No. 602 Squadron, 12 Spitfires, to Kenley–Biggin Hill–Gravesend area.
No. 10 Group		
2.28	Middle Wallop	No. 609 Squadron, 13 Spitfires, to Brooklands–Kenley area at 15,000 feet.

UXBRIDGE, 2.20 P.M. As reports of the initial clash reached Park's headquarters the commander ordered off his last two day-fighter units, Nos 303 and 602 Squadrons. Now all twenty-one of his Spitfire and Hurricane squadrons were airborne, and either in contact with the enemy or moving into position to engage. From No. 12 Group, Squadron Leader Douglas Bader was again on his way south at the head of the five-squadron Big Wing. And from the west two squadrons from No. 10 Group were moving towards the capital.

For the defence of London a total of 276 Spitfires and Hurricanes were now airborne, slightly more than for the earlier engagement. But this German raiding force was more than twice as large as the earlier one, outnumbering the British fighters by more than two to one. For every two Spitfires or Hurricanes airborne, three Messerschmitt 109s were now running in over Kent.

ABOVE TENTERDEN, 2.20 P.M. The second wave of fighters to engage the raiders comprised Nos 607 and 213 Squadrons, with twenty-three Hurricanes. Their arrival took the escorts by surprise and before they could intervene Squadron Leader J. Vick led a head-on charge into the Dorniers of Bomber Geschwader 3.

With the two formations closing at a combined speed of about 450 m.p.h. the risk of collision was considerable. Pilot Officer Paddy Stephenson of No. 607 Squadron loosed off a short burst at one of the Dorniers and was about to pull up to pass close over the top of his target when he saw that his escape route was blocked by another Hurricane. He explained to the author: 'Our squadron was flying in four Vics, in stepped-down formation.

The bombers were flying in stepped-up formation. In a head-on attack each Vic was supposed to pass above the aircraft being attacked, and immediately below the following bomber. To do this there needed to be a proper spacing between the Vics in our squadron. My Vic had moved too far forward and to break away upwards would have involved me in a crash with a Hurricane in the leading Vic of our formation.' Stephenson made a split-second decision: if a collision there had to be, it was preferable to hit a foe rather than a friend.

The impact followed almost immediately. Stephenson's starboard wing struck the starboard wing of one of the Dorniers, shattering both. Horst Schulz had watched the approaching Hurricanes growing rapidly larger in front of him, wings blinking as they opened fire. 'The next moment there was an explosion in front of me, then pieces of planes were falling out of the sky like confetti. I didn't know whether a British fighter had collided with one of our planes, or if it had suffered a direct hit from flak. There was no time to brood about it, I had my own job to do.'

After the collision the Hurricane reared up, rolled on its back and went down in a steep inverted dive. Only after a lot of kicking, in the course of which he broke an ankle, was Stephenson able to fight his way out of his cockpit and jump clear.

Meanwhile the shattered Dornier was also spinning out of control. Penned in their cabin by the vicious G forces, the terrified crew were still inside the bomber when it plunged into a small wood near Kilndown.

The battle around the bombers continued, as the Hurricanes split into sections and curved round to join the Spitfires attempting to engage the bombers from astern and from the flanks. Again and again the Messerschmitts came diving in to break up attacks or drive away Spitfires or Hurricanes. For their part the bomber crews held tight formation and put up a powerful cross-fire whenever a British fighter came within range.

For the pilots of Messerschmitts assigned to the close escort this was a particularly frustrating time. They were not permitted to pursue enemy fighters and go for a kill if that meant leaving their charges. Again and again the Messerschmitts had to break off the chase and return to their bombers. Then the British fighters would return and the process would be repeated.

Next to join the mêlée around the bombers were Nos 605 and

501 Squadrons, with fourteen Hurricanes. And now, four minutes after the loss of its first Dornier in collision, Bomber Geschwader 3 would lose another to this cause. As Pilot Officer Tom Cooper-Slipper closed fast on a Dornier in the leading element, an accurate burst struck his fighter, 'I was left with only partial control over my plane. I knew I was going to have to bail out, so I decided to ram the Dornier first. I struck the bomber from three-quarters rear and I saw the Dornier slew round in front of me. My overtaking speed was about 50 m.p.h. and I was surprised at the small force of the impact.' Despite the small impact force, the collision wrecked both aircraft. Minus part of the port wing, the Hurricane tumbled out of the sky in a violent spin. Cooper-Slipper struggled to open his canopy but at first it refused to budge. Finally he managed to slide it back and jump clear, then he passed out. The next thing the fighter pilot knew he was floating down beneath his parachute. He had no recollection of having pulled the ripcord. Meanwhile, the Dornier was also going down fast and its crew were also bailing out.

Dumbfounded, Horst Schulz watched it all happen: 'The British fighter came in from right to left, from the rear, and rammed into the Dornier. Then I saw three parachutes appear from the two aircraft as they went down. But again I could not spend much time watching, I had to hold formation or I would be joining them . . .'

Those in the Dorniers who had observed the two collisions had no way of knowing that neither had been premeditated. To some of the watchers it seemed that the Royal Air Force might be in such desperate straits that its pilots had orders to ram the bombers. If this was the case, the tactic was devastatingly effective. Chastened by the losses, the Dornier crews adjusted formation to close the gaps and continued determinedly toward their target.

CHATHAM, 2.31 P.M. Following the initial attacks on the bombers, the escorts re-grouped. Again the action devolved into a series of short, fleeting combats between the opposing fighters. The respite for the German bomber crews would be brief, however, for soon afterwards they came within range of the anti-aircraft batteries deployed along the Thames. Initially the presence of British fighters in the vicinity of the bombers, and the near-continuous blanket cloud, prevented the gunners engaging. Then the fighters pulled clear, the bombers entered a clear patch and the gunners had their chance. From sites to the south and west of Chatham, a concentration of twenty 4.5-in. and eight 3.7-in. guns opened up a heavy cannonade.

Once again the Dorniers of Bomber Geschwader 3 were on the receiving end. The bombers immediately began a 'flak waltz' to avoid the enemy fire. Feldwebel Heinz Kirsch, a gunner in one of the bombers, recalled: 'Suddenly flak bursts appeared beneath us; ugly black puffs about 600 metres below. We had to be getting near London.'

The formation's snake-like flight path enabled it to circumvent most of the flak bursts, but not all of them. Leutnant Herburt Michaelis felt his Dornier reel as if it had been struck by some huge invisible fist, then the port engine ground to a halt. Unable to keep up with his comrades, the German pilot swung away from the formation and headed for the skein of clouds below.

The Heinkels of Bomber Geschwader 53, comprising the centre column of the attack force, were next to come within range of the gunners. Oberleutnant Peter Schierning, a navigator in nose of one of the bombers, could just make out the distant smudge of London behind the thinning smoke puffs left from the previous engagement. Then lumps of sky around the bomber suddenly turned black as more shells burst, much closer and more threatening. In an instant the sky was clear and the smoke and stench of the explosions were left behind, but the damage had been done. 'One of the first salvoes knocked out our right motor,' Schierning recalled. 'We felt no shock, but the motor slowly wound down. The pilot shouted "Get rid of the bombs! Get rid of the bombs! I can't hold it!" I jettisoned the bombs over farm land.' Also unable to keep up with its formation, the bomber curved for the protection of cloud.

UXBRIDGE, 2.35 P.M. Fifteen minutes after the last of his day-fighter squadrons had taken off, Air Vice-Marshal Park's force was now at full stretch. Several units were in contact with the enemy and others were converging on the raiders from all directions. Describing the unfolding pattern of the events in the operations room, Winston Churchill would later write:

> I became conscious of the anxiety of the Commander, who now stood still behind his subordinate's chair. Hitherto I had watched

in silence. I now asked: 'What other reserves have we?' 'There are none,' said Air Vice-Marshal Park. In an account which he wrote about it afterwards he said that at this I 'looked grave'. Well I might. What loses should we not suffer if our refuelling planes were caught on the ground by further raids of '40 plus' or '50 plus'! The odds were great; our margins small; the stakes infinite.

The situation concerning reserves was indeed grave. At Park's request, Nos 10 and 12 Groups had sent to the capital every Spitfire and Hurricane squadron from those sectors immediately adjacent to No. 11 Group. If the Germans were now to launch a follow-up attack, only three squadrons were available to meet it and none was well placed to go into action over Kent or the capital. No. 12 Group had a squadron of Spitfires at readiness at Coltishall in Norfolk, and No. 10 Group had a squadron of Spitfires at Warmwell in Dorset and one of Hurricanes at Boscombe Down in Wiltshire. All three airfields were more than a hundred miles from London, however, and the fighters would take at least half an hour to get there following the order to scramble. All the other day-fighter squadrons were based too far from the capital to play any effective part in the fighting there.

Keith Park was an astute commander and there is little doubt that he had weighed the risks carefully before getting into this position. On the wall of his operations room, beside the tote boards giving the status of each of his squadrons, were boards showing the weather – and in particular the cloud cover – at the main fighter airfields:

Croydon – 8/10 cumulus and strato-cumulus, base 2,000 ft
Hornchurch – 6/10 cumulus and strato-cumulus, base 3,000 ft
Northolt – 9/10 cumulus, base 3,500 ft
Hendon – 9/10 cumulus, base 2,100 ft
Biggin Hill – 9/10 cumulus and strato-cumulus, base 2,000 ft

Thus the No. 11 Group commander knew that the almost-complete blanket of cloud over his airfields made accurate high-altitude attacks on them improbable. Almost certainly this had influenced his decision to commit all of his Spitfire and Hurricane squadrons.

At about this time one squadron of Spitfires and two of Hurricanes, units that had been among the first to go into action, broke away and headed for base. These squadrons (Nos 41, 213 and 605) had been airborne for less than three-quarters of an hour, and their fighters had plenty of fuel though some were low

Air Chief Marshal Hugh Dowding, C-in-C Fighter Command, escorting the King and Queen during their visit to his headquarters at Bentley Priory north of London early in September 1940. (IWM)

Air Vice-Marshal Keith Park commanded No 11 Group of Fighter Command, which bore the brunt of the fighting during the September actions in defence of London. (IWM)

Scenes inside No 11 Group's operations room. *Above*, the plotting table seen from the command gallery. *Below*, the command gallery seen from the floor of the room.

(*Above*) The author standing beside the memorial plaque near the entrance to the underground operations room at Uxbridge, from which Air Vice-Marshal Park directed No 11 Group in the defence of London on 15 September 1940. Winston Churchill was visiting Park's headquarters that day.

(*Below*) Ex-Luftwaffe aircrew and their wives pictured during a post-war visit to the No 11 Group operations room. Lord Willoughby de Broke (Park's senior controller on 15 September) with pointer, is explaining the fighter control process to his one-time enemies. Immediately to the left of de Broke, without a tie, is Wilhelm Raab and standing above him on the dais is Theodor Rehm; both flew with Bomber Geschwader 76 during the attack on London.

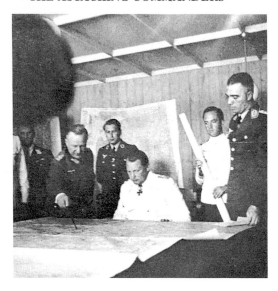

(*Above*) Goering pictured at a planning conference. On the far right is Oberst Josef Schmid, head of the Luftwaffe Intelligence Directorate, who calculated that RAF Fighter Command was on its last legs by 15 September. (*Below*) Generalfeldmarschall Hugo Sperrle, right, the commander of Air Fleet 3.

(*Above*) Reichsmarschall Herman Goering in conversation with Adolf Hitler. Between them is Grand Admiral Erich Raeder, responsible for the naval planning of the invasion of England.
(*Below*) Generalfeldmarschall Albert Kesselring commanded Air Fleet 2 which mounted the two large scale attacks on London on 15 September.

(*Above*) The crew boarding a Heinkel 111 of Bomber Geschwader 4, one of the units that attacked London during the early morning darkness of 15 September. The aircraft carries an external load of two 2,200 pound bombs, weapons similar to the one that landed beside St Paul's Cathedral and failed to detonate.

(*Above*) Pilot Officer Dennis David of No 87 Squadron took part in the destruction of the first German aircraft to go down on 15 September. The aircraft, a Heinkel on a weather reconnaissance mission, was intercepted near Salcombe during the early morning, and crashed into the sea. There were no survivors. (Dennis David)

(*Above*) A troop of four 3.7-in anti-aircraft guns firing from Hyde Park. Although the guns destroyed few night bombers, and none on 15 September, these weapons were usually successful in forcing the raiders to attack from altitudes above 16,000 feet with a consequent reduction in bombing accuracy. Also the noise of guns firing and shells exploding provided the shadow, if not the substance, of an effective air defence for those living in the capital. (Central Press)

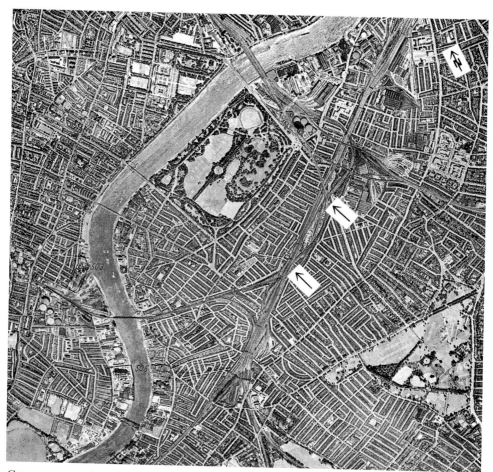

German reconnaissance photograph taken eleven days before the action on 15 September, showing the rail viaducts in Battersea (arrowed) attacked by Bomber Geschwader 76 during the noon action. Battersea Park and the Thames can be seen to the north of the rail network.

Major Alois Lindmayer, commander of the IIIrd Gruppe of Bomber Geschwader 76, led the noon attack on London. Shortage of fuel forced the escorting Me 109s to turn for home just short of the city, but Lindmayer and his bombers continued with the attack. Afterwards he conducted a brilliant fighting withdrawal under attack from twelve squadrons of British fighters. (Rehm)

Dornier 17 of Bomber Geschwader 76 releasing a stick of 110 pound bombs.

'Bombs on Britain' insignia worn by Dornier 17s of 2nd Staffel of Bomber Geschwader 76. (KG 76 Archive)

Taken on the morning of 15 September, this photograph shows a Bomber Geschwader 76 crew at Beauvais before setting out for London. From left to right: Feldwebel Niebler (pilot), Oberleutnant Wilke (navigator), Feldwebel Wissmann (gunner), ground crewman, Unteroffizier Schatz (engineer/gunner) and Unteroffizier Zrenner (radio operator/gunner). Just over two hours later their Dornier was shot down by British fighters and crashed near Sturry. Wilke and Zrenner bailed out and were taken prisoner, the others were killed. (Rehm)

Flight Lieutenant Ken Gillies of No 66 Squadron, in the cockpit of his Spitfire, was one of those who shared in the destruction of Niebler's bomber. Gillies was killed in action early in October. (*The Times*)

(*Left*) Air test of the flame thrower fitted to Rolf Heitsch's Dornier. The 'secret weapon' made its operational debut during the noon action, but as a deterrent to fighter attack it proved a complete failure. (Heitsch)

(*Middle picture*) Feldwebel Heitsch's Dornier pictured after its crash landing near Sevenoaks, being dismantled by an RAF team before removal. (via Cornwell)

(*Bottom picture*) Rolf Heitsch describing to the author the action in which his bomber was shot down by enemy fighters.

(*Left*) Its tail knocked off when it was rammed by Ray Holmes's Hurricane, the Dornier flipped on to its back and both outer wing panels broke away. Then the bomber fell out of the sky in a vicious spin. Holmes's fighter is also seen diving towards the ground, out of control.

(*Right*) The tail of the Dornier descending on London.

The main part of the Dornier spinning to earth, moments before it impacted beside Victoria Station. (IWM)

Sergeant Ray Holmes of No 501 Squadron, who was fortunate to escape with his life after ramming the Dornier.

(*Above and right*) The engines and the main part of the wreckage of the rammed Dornier came down on the forecourt of Victoria Station, between the main station building and a gift shop. (via Cornwell)

On the roof of a public house in Vauxhall Bridge Road, soldiers examine the severed tail of the bomber. (via Cornwell)

Bomb damage caused to bridges and rail lines passing through Battersea during the noon attack. (National Railway Museum)

Feldwebel Wilhelm Raab of Bomber Geschwader 76 (*above*) was attacked by several British fighters during the noon action on 15 September and finished off by Flight Lieutenant Peter Brothers of No 257 Squadron (*below left*). Both men had narrow escapes with death on that day. They are seen (*below right*) after they were brought together by the author during the research for this book. (Raab, Brothers)

Squadron Leader Douglas Bader (*left*), the famous fighter leader who had had both legs amputated following an air crash before the war, led the five-squadron 'Big Wing' from No 12 Group into action over London at noon on 15 September. (IWM)

Spitfire pilots of No 19 Squadron (*centre*) that saw action that day. From left to right: Plt Off 'Jock' Cunningham, Sub-Lieutenant 'The Admiral' Blake (seconded from the Fleet Air Arm), Flt Lt F. Dolezal from Czechoslovakia and Fg Off F. Brinsden from New Zealand. (No 19 Squadron Archive)

(*Right*) Hurricane pilots of No 302 (Polish) Squadron. From left to right: unidentified, Sgt A. Beda, Fg Off T. Czerwinski, Plt Off W. Gnys, Plt Off B. Bernas, Plt Off S. Chalupa. The squadron went into action for the first time on 15 September. (Cynk)

Unteroffizier Figge of Bomber Geschwader 76 (right) crash landed his Dornier near Poix after it was badly shot up over London during the noon action. The aircraft returned to France on one engine. (Rehm)

(*Left and below*) Other shots of Figge's Dornier. The crewman wearing the field dressing swigging at the bottle is Oberleutnant Florian, the navigator. (Rehm)

Close-up of the wing to Figge's aircraft. On the original print more than fifty bullet hits are visible. The plane was damaged beyond repair. (Rehm)

Unteroffizier Theordor Rehm (right) and his crew after their return to Beauvais following the noon attack on London. Their aircraft had collected 47 hits; note the shot-out tyre on the port wheel. (Rehm)

THE BOMB BESIDE ST PAUL'S CATHEDRAL

While sappers were digging down to the unexploded bomb beside St Paul's Cathedral, dropped during the early morning darkness on the 12th, the surrounding area was evacuated. This photograph was taken looking east along Ludgate Hill, and the bomb was buried next to the clock tower to the right of the dome. (Central Press)

The top of the shaft beside the south-west corner of the Cathedral. More than 70 tons of soil had to be dug out by hand to reach the bomb, which was 27 feet below ground. The bomb was extracted at mid-day on 15 September, driven to Hackney Marshes and exploded. (IWM)

Messerschmitt 109s of Fighter Geschwader 53 about to take off from Wissant, prior to a mission against England. The Geschwader supported both attacks on London on 15 September.

Oberleutnant Hans Schmoller-Haldy (facing camera) pictured with pilots of Fighter Geschwader 54 at the officer's mess at Campagne during the Battle of Britain. Schmoller-Haldy piloted an Me 109 escorting Heinkels of Bomber Geschwader 26 during the afternoon attack on London. (Schmoller-Haldy)

Major Adolf Galland, the commander of Fighter Geschwader 26, pictured in his personal Me 109. Galland scored his 33rd aerial victory during the afternoon action, when he shot down Sergeant J. Hubacek of No 310 Squadron; the latter bailed out with minor injuries. (via Schliephake)

TARGETS

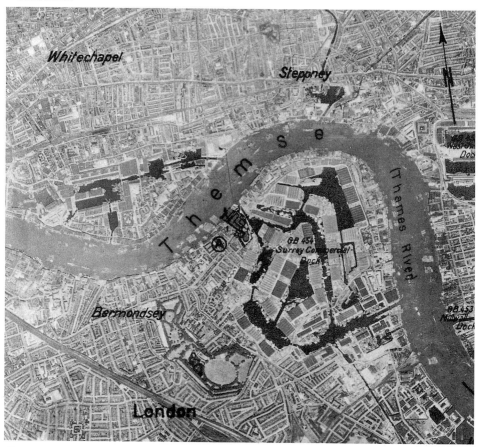

German target photograph of the Surrey Commercial Docks, the planned objective for the Dorniers of Bomber Geschwader 2.

German reconnaissance photograph of the West Ham and Stepney areas of London. The Bromley-by-Bow gasworks, arrowed, was hit hard during the afternoon attack.

When his Hurricane was seriously damaged by return fire from Dorniers of Bomber Geschwader 3, Pilot Officer Tom Cooper-Slipper of No 605 Squadron decided to ram one of the bombers. Both aircraft were destroyed; Cooper-Slipper and three out of the four German crewmen parachuted to safety. (T. Cooper-Slipper)

Pilot Officer Alan Wright of No 19 Squadron flew his Spitfire on a Spotter mission over mid-Channel, to report on the strength and composition of the incoming raiding force. He was the first to make contact with the enemy during the afternoon action. (Wright)

Pilots of No 504 Squadron. From left to right: Squadron Leader John Sample, Plt Off Mike Rook, Fg Off 'Scruffy Royce', Sgt 'Wag' Haw. (via Severnside Aviation Society)

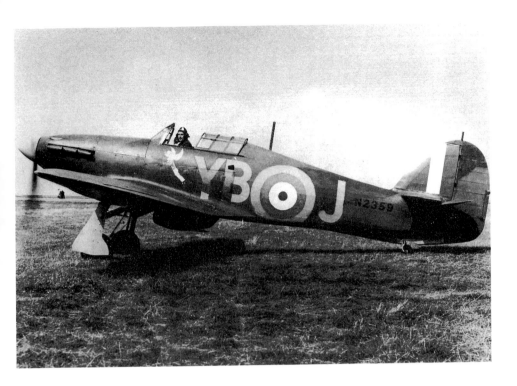

(*Above*) Pilot Officer L. Stevens of No 17 Squadron in his Hurricane and (*below*) Pilot Officer 'Pedro' Hanbury of No 602 Squadron in his Spitfire. Both pilots took part in actions near London during the afternoon of the 15th.

Oberleutnant Peter Schierning of Bomber Geschwader 53 was taken prisoner after his He 111 was shot down by several British fighters near Staplehurst. (Schierning)

A Heinkel 111 releasing a stick of 110-pound bombs. These small weapons were housed in the bomb bay nose-up, and tumbled away from the aircraft after release.

Heinkel 111s in attack formation.

Abschuss über England 15.9.1940.14 Gesunde gegen 1.Kranken!

Cartoon, drawn by Schierning during his captivity, with a not-too-serious view of the action in which he was shot down. (Schierning)

Dornier 17s of IInd Gruppe of Bomber Geschwader 3, the unit that suffered the heaviest loss rate of those that took part in the day's fighting: of nineteen aircraft that crossed the coast of England six (31 per cent) were shot down. Many of the others suffered damage. (Schultz)

Feldwebel Horst Schultz brought his Dornier home on one engine, and was accompanied to the coast of Kent by a British fighter. (Schultz)

Leutnant Schopper crash-landed his seriously damaged Dornier on sand-dunes near Dunkirk. He stands on the left of the group. Feldwebel Heinz Kirsch, whose account appears in this book, is second from the left. (Kirsch)

Pilot Officer Peter Pease of No 603 Squadron carried out a courageous single-handed attack on a formation of Heinkels during the afternoon action, but was shot down by Messerschmitts immediately afterwards and died when his blazing Spitfire crashed near Maidstone. (Sir Richard Pease)

The Heinkel piloted by Oberleutnant Roderich Cescotti of Bomber Geschwader 26 suffered damage during the attack by Pease. (Cescotti)

Unteroffizier Hermann Streibing of Lehrgeschwader 2 had a narrow escape when he bailed out of his Me 109 at low altitude. His half-open parachute caught on the chimney of a house. (Streibing)

Sergeant Don Mackay, Royal Artillery, helped Streibing to the ground and took him prisoner. (Mackay)

(*Below*) More than 40 years after the incident Don Mackay (right) shows Streibing the house on which the latter came down. (Mackay)

A troop of four 4.5-in guns of No 52 Heavy Anti-Aircraft Regiment, Royal Artillery, near Barking. This unit was one of several that engaged German bombers during the afternoon action. The 4.5-in was the heaviest of anti-aircraft weapon used during the day's fighting, and fired 55-pound shells at a maximum rate of eight per minute. (IWM)

Gunners of No 166 Battery, No 55 Heavy Anti-Aircraft Regiment, at Fort Borstal near Chatham. The fin and rudder come from the Dornier of Bomber Geschwader 2 in whose destruction they assisted and which crashed into a nearby house. (McMachan)

(*Left*) Messerschmitt 110 fighter-bombers of
Erprobungsgruppe 210. Late in the afternoon ten of
these aircraft attempted to bomb the Supermarine
Aircraft Works at Woolston on the outskirts of
Southampton where Spitfires were built.

Right) Ground crewmen of Epr.
r. 210 awaiting the order to load
0-pounders on the unit's
esserschmitts.

elow) Bomb damage near
oolston station, after the
erman fighter-bombers missed
eir target. (Southern
ewspapers)

During the daylight hours of 15 September, unarmed Spitfires of the Photographic Reconnaissance Unit flew from Heston near London to every large port between Antwerp and Cherbourg, to observe invasion preparations.

Unteroffizier Walburger's Messerschmitt 109 crash-landed near Uckfield after being shot down during the noon action on 15 September. His aircraft is seen some weeks later beside the boarded-up Nelson's Column in Trafalgar Square, where it was placed on exhibition as part of a national savings drive. (via Cornwell)

on ammunition. It is speculation on the author's part, but it appears likely that Park had ordered these squadrons to return early to refuel and rearm, in order to re-create a fighting reserve as soon as possible.

As during the noon action, Park now concentrated the bulk of his force for the main action immediately in front of London. No fewer than nineteen fresh squadrons were being vectored into position (Nos 1 RCAF, 17, 19, 46, 66, 72, 73, 229, 238, 242, 249, 253, 257, 302, 303, 310, 504, 603, and 611) with a total of 185 Spitfires and Hurricanes.

The action about to begin would involve about five hundred aircraft. In this narrative the actions around each of the three German bomber columns will be described separately, though in fact they took place simultaneously.

GRAVESEND AREA, 2.35 P.M. The right-hand column of raiders comprised the Dorniers of Bomber Geschwader 3, followed by the Heinkels of Bomber Geschwader 26. Yet again the leading element of this column would bear the brunt of the attack, this time from sixty-three fighters from six squadrons (Nos 17, 46, 249, 257, 504 and 603).

Among the first to go into action during this phase were the Hurricanes of Nos 249 and 504 Squadrons. Pilot Officer Tom Neil, with the former unit, would later write:

> We were not far removed from the scene of our fight in the morning when some 109s flew across out heads several thousand feet higher. The harbingers of trouble! Then, the familiar ack-ack and line of bombers. Dorniers again. We were about the same height and not badly positioned. We curved towards them, climbing slightly.
>
> The Dorniers – I counted seven or eight of them in the nearest group – were in a broad vic and I mentally resolved not to fly into the middle of the formation and risk being shot to pieces by rear-gunner crossfire. Instead, I concentrated on an aircraft out on the right and, everything clicking into place, found myself dead astern, just below it and pitching about in its slipstream.
>
> Closing, I fired immediately and the whole of the port side of the German aircraft was engulfed in my tracer. The effect was instantaneous; there was a splash of something like water being struck with the back of a spoon. Beside myself with excitement, I fired again, a longish burst, and finding that I was too close, fell back a little but kept my position.

Then, astonishingly, before I was ready to renew my assault, two large objects detached themselves from the fuselage and came in my direction, so quickly, in fact, that I had no time to evade. Comprehension barely keeping pace with events, I suddenly recognized spreadeagled arms and legs as two bodies flew past my head, heavy with the bulges that were undeveloped parachutes. The crew! Baling out! I veered away, shocked by what I had just achieved.

Almost certainly the bomber Neil had hit was that bearing Hauptmann Ernst Puettmann, the commander of 5th Staffel of Bomber Geschwader 3 and leader of the formation, which went down into the Thames Estuary at this time after two of the crew bailed out. Meanwhile, high above the river, the action continued around Neil:

> But I had little time in which to dwell on the matter as I was immediately engulfed by 109s which swept over my head and turned towards me venomously, clearly intent on murder.
>
> I have no recollection of what precisely I did except that, in a frenzy of self-preservation, I pulled and pushed and savagely yanked my aircraft about, firing whenever I caught sight of a wing or a fuselage in my windscreen. They were not sighted bursts, just panic hosings designed to scare rather than kill and directed against aircraft that were often within yards of me. For all of, what? – twenty seconds? A murderous, desperate interlude.
>
> Then, as so often happened, they were gone and I was alone. Not alone, exactly, but not immediately threatened. There were perhaps half a dozen aircraft visible in that vast arena of clouds and space in which I was a single moving dot.

Heinz Kirsch, in one of the Dorniers attacked during this engagement, described the action from the German side:

> A new call, 'Fighters dead astern!' Something struck our machine. 'Hit on the left elevator!' called the radio operator. Like a couple of shadows two Hurricanes swept over us. They came past so quickly we were unable to 'greet' them. More hits on our machine. And on top of that there was smoke in the cabin. The Tommies were staking everything they had, never before had we come under such heavy attack. After firing, the fighters pulled left or right to go past us. Some came so close I thought they were going to ram us.

During the attack three Dorniers were knocked out of formation. From his Me 109 Hans Schmoller-Haldy, flying close escort to the Heinkels coming up behind, watched them go down: 'There were parachutes all over the place. Several British fighters were buzzing around the Dorniers. I thought "Oh, those poor men . . ." But we couldn't do anything to help, we had to stay with our Heinkels.' Moments later Schmoller-Haldy and his comrades had their work cut out, as Squadron Leader Stanford Tuck led nine Hurricanes of No. 257 Squadron in an attempt to punch through to the Heinkels.

THE CENTRE COLUMN, the Heinkels of Bomber Geschwader 53, came under attack from forty-one fighters (Nos 1 RCAF, 66, 72 and 229 Squadrons). Squadron Leader Rupert Leigh led nine Spitfires of No. 66 Squadron in a head-on attack, while two 'weavers' provided top cover to hold off any Messerschmitts that might attempt to interfere. Flight Lieutenant Bob Oxspring, in one of the covering Spitfires, recalled: 'While the others went in to attack, I was a bit concerned about some Me 109s above me and did a 360 degree turn to ward them off. I climbed to get more altitude in case there was a fight, being careful not to lose speed in the process . . . never get caught by the enemy at climbing speed, that is the worst thing that can happen.'

While Oxspring kept a wary eye on the enemy fighters, Leigh ordered the other Spitfires into line astern, went into a shallow dive to build up speed, then pulled up steeply to attack the Heinkels from in front and below – the quarter where their defensive armament was weakest. Spitfire after Spitfire ran in to short range, fired a brief burst then broke away. High above, Bob Oxspring watched the Messerschmitts continue on unconcernedly. 'They did not seem about to interfere so I went down after the rest of the squadron and attacked one of the bombers from out of the sun. With .303-in. ammunition you never knew if you had hit an enemy aircraft, unless you saw a flash or some obvious form of damage. The Heinkel broke away from the formation. I continued on, going down fast, and went through the formation.'

Next the Spitfires of No. 72 Squadron attacked, followed by the Hurricanes of Nos 1 (Canadian) and 229 Squadrons. One of the bombers caught a lethal burst, it is not clear from whom. The shattered machine fell out of the sky like a fireball trailing sparks, and smashed into open ground at Woolwich Arsenal. There were no survivors. Two more Heinkels, less seriously damaged, were forced to turn for home.

The Ist Gruppe of Fighter Geschwader 3 had nine Me 109s providing close escort for these Heinkels. The unit's war diary describes an attack by British fighters on the bombers, probably that by No. 66 Squadron: 'The Spitfires approached the bombers in the climb from below, fired, and dived away. Hptm von Hahn shot down 1 Spitfire, Lt Rohwer 1 Hurricane.'

These Geman claims relate to the Spitfire of No. 66 Squadron and the Hurricane of No. 1 (Canadian) Squadron damaged during that engagement. Flying Officer Yuile, the pilot of the latter, later commented:

> We were diving in to attack a formation of Heinkels. I was so intent on watching the bombers that I forgot for a moment that we were supposed to have eyes in the side and back of our heads, as well as in front. A Messerschmitt that I had failed to notice flashed down on my tail and the next thing I knew something hit me in the shoulder with the force of a sledgehammer. An armour piercing bullet had penetrated the armour plate of the cockpit and got me. I was momentarily numbed, and when I swung round the German had gone.

Yuile broke off the action and headed for Northolt.

THE LEFT-HAND COLUMN of the raiding force, with two separate formations of Dorniers from Bomber Geschwader 2, came under attack from twenty-three Hurricanes (Nos 73, 253 and 303 Squadrons). The escorts were active, however, and prevented the Hurricanes from delivering concerted attacks. One of the Me 109 pilots, Unteroffizier Koppenschlaeger of Fighter Geschwader 53, became separated from his comrades, so he climbed to 26,000 feet above the Dorniers: 'Suddenly I saw beneath me a Spitfire moving into position to attack a Do 17. I dived into an attacking position, and after a short burst pieces broke off the Spitfire's wing. The Spitfire burst into flames and, burning, dived vertically into cloud.' The evidence is not conclusive, but it appears the 'Spitfire' was in fact a Hurricane of No. 303 Squadron shot down at this time. The Polish pilot, Sergeant Andruszkow, parachuted safely. Andruszkow's squadron was heavily engaged by Messerschmitts during this phase of the action and lost another Hurricane destroyed and five more damaged.

Meanwhile, Sergeant Garton and at least one other pilot of No. 73 Squadron succeeded in delivering a frontal attack on the

Dorniers. Garton saw his rounds stitching into one of the bombers, then it emitted a puff of white smoke and edged away from the formation.

Oberleutnant Werner Kittmann was navigator in that Dornier. 'The first thing I knew about the British fighters was when I saw two of them coming straight towards me. I had been looking through my bombsight and did not have time to get to my machine gun and fire at them. The attack damaged our left engine, which lost oil and began to run rough. We dropped out of the formation and turned for home.'

DOUGLAS BADER'S 'Big Wing' had been scrambled too late, and now its pilots would have to pay the price for that error. The five squadrons arrived over London still in the climb and almost immediately came under attack from above by free-hunting Me 109s. Bader ordered the three Hurricane squadrons to split up and engage the enemy fighters while, in a reversal of their usual role, the Spitfires were to try to get through to the bombers. Bader's own combat report described the chaos that now ensued:

> On being attacked from behind by Me 109 I ordered break up and pulled up and round violently. Coming off my back partially blacked out, nearly collided with Yellow 2 [Pilot Officer Crowley-Milling]. Spun off his slipstream and straightened out 5,000 feet below without firing a shot. Climbed up again and saw E/A twin engined flying westwards. Just got in range and fired a short burst (3 secs) in a completely stalled position and then spun off again and lost more height.

The 'Big Wing' was unable to deliver the hoped-for concerted attack on a bomber formation. But, by its presence, the Wing engaged the attention of several of the enemy free-hunting patrols, making it easier for other British squadrons to reach the bombers.

AT THIS TIME there were numerous violent and confused fights between the opposing fighters. Few manoeuvring combats lasted more than about twenty seconds, however: any pilot concentrating his attention too long on one enemy fighter ran the risk of being blasted out of the sky by another. On this day the author has found only *one* recorded instance of a protracted combat between individual fighters. Squadron Leader Brian Lane, leading No. 19 Squadron with Spitfires, had come south with Douglas Bader's Wing. When the Wing was split up, Lane was attacked by an Me 109. He avoided the enemy fire, then curved after the Messerschmitt to deliver his riposte:

> He saw me as I turned after him and, putting on full inside rudder as he turned, skidded underneath me. Pulling round half stalled, I tore after him and got in a short burst as I closed on him before he was out of my sights again. That German pilot certainly knew how to handle a 109 – I have never seen one thrown about as that one was, and I felt certain that his wings would come off at any moment. However, they stayed on, and he continued to lead me a hell of a dance as I strove to get my sights on him again. Twice I managed to get in a short burst but I don't think I hit him, then he managed to get round towards my tail. Pulling hard round I started to gain on him and began to come round towards his tail. He was obviously turning as tightly as his kite could and I could see that his slots [on the leading edge of the wings] were open, showing he was nearly stalled. His ailerons were obviously snatching too, as first one wing and then the other would dip violently.
>
> Giving the Spitfire best, he suddenly flung out of the turn and rolled right over on his back passing across in front of me inverted. I couldn't quite see the point of this manoeuvre unless he hoped I would roll after him, when, knowing no doubt that my engine would cut [because of the float-type carburetter fitted to the Merlin engine] whereas his was still going, owing to his petrol injection system, he would draw away from me. Either that or he blacked out and didn't realize what was happening for a moment, for he flew on inverted for several seconds, giving me the chance to get in a good burst from the quarter. Half righting himself for a moment, he slowly dived down and disappeared into the clouds still upside down, looking very much out of control.
>
> The sweat was pouring down my face and my oxygen mask was wet and sticky about my nose and mouth. I felt quite exhausted after the effort and my right arm ached from throwing the stick around the cockpit. At speed it needs quite a bit of exertion to move the stick quickly and coarsely in violent manoeuvres.

Afterwards Lane would claim the Me 109 'probably destroyed'. This claim does not link with any known German loss, however, and no Me 109 came down on land within twenty miles of Dartford where the combat was reported to have taken place.

As has been said, long manoeuvring combats were a rarity. More usually, fighter pilots engaging their enemy counterparts would follow the adage 'get in fast, hit hard, get out'. Over the

Thames Estuary that afternoon the commander of Fighter Geschwader 26, Major Adolf Galland, gave a masterly display of this type of attack:

> After an unsuccessful ten-minute dogfight with about eight Hurricanes, during which much altitude was lost, with the Staff flight I attacked two Hurricanes about 800 m. below us. Maintaining surprise, I closed on the wing man and opened fire from 120 m. as he was in a gentle turn to the left. The enemy plane reeled as my rounds struck the nose from below, and pieces fell from the left wing and fuselage. The left side of the fuselage burst into flame. The enemy section leader was shot down in flames by my wing man, Oberleutnant Horten.

The Hurricanes belonged to No. 310 (Czech) Squadron. Galland's victory, his 33rd, had followed a classic surprise attack from his victim's blind zone. The subsequent report of the Hurricane pilot, Sergeant J. Hubacek, makes it clear that he never even saw his assailant.

> '. . . I climbed again and at about 18,000 ft I had the impression that I heard machine-gun fire behind me. I looked back several times but I did not see anything. I re-trimmed the aircraft, but at that moment I was hit – I do not know by what – the cockpit was full of smoke but I did not see any fire. The aircraft turned first to the right and then went slowly into a spin.

Hubacek bailed out and landed with injuries to his right foot.

Squadron Leader A. Hess parachuted from the Hurricane that Horten shot down, and landed without injury. Both British fighters crashed near Billericay.

EASTERN OUTSKIRTS OF LONDON, 2.40 P.M. Now the German bomber formations were about to start their bombing runs. On the way to the target the right-hand column of bombers had lost three Dorniers destroyed, and two Dorniers and a Heinkel forced to turn back. From the central column a Heinkel had been destroyed and three more forced to turn back, and from the left-hand column one Dornier had been forced to turn back. But despite the depredations of the defences, just over a hundred German bombers had reached the capital and the 120 tons of bombs they carried could inflict severe damage. The afternoon action was about to enter its critical phase.

During the approach of the German formations over Kent, cloud had hindered tracking and made it difficult for the British controllers to direct their fighters with precision. Now those same banks of cloud were to shield London's dock areas from the bombs intended for them. Like Park's fighter bases, most of the capital was enshrouded by nine-tenths cumulus and strato-cumulus cloud with its base at about 2,000 feet and the tops extending to 12,000 feet.

The German bombers in the right and centre columns arrived over the capital to find the Royal Victoria Docks and their other briefed targets enshrouded in cloud. There were clear skies over West Ham, however, just beyond their intended targets. The Dorniers and Heinkels realigned their bombing runs on the borough.

As the bomber formations reached the area of clear sky over East Ham, they came into view of the anti-aircraft batteries deployed there and the gunners opened up a vigorous and accurate fire. From his Dornier, Heinz Kirsch watched the Thames slide beneath him: 'More flak bursts, some of them damn' near. We could feel the concussion from the exploding shells, an uncomfortable feeling. Then at last came the call "Bomb doors open".'

When the gunners opened fire several British fighters were milling around the bombers, and the Spitfires and Hurricanes maintained contact despite the bursting shells. To the German crews this looked like one more sign of the enemy's reckless determination to defend the capital, at any cost. An official Luftwaffe report on this phase of the action later commented: 'The [enemy] fighters pressed home their attacks either singly or in pairs, without regard for the flak . . .' The British side of the story is rather different. In accordance with laid-down pro-cedure, as the fighter pilots ran in to attack they expected the gunners to cease fire immediately. That did not happen and afterwards there would be bitter complaints. Flying Officer B. MacNamara of No. 603 Squadron, for example, stated in his official report: 'Throughout this attack I was troubled by heavy AA fire, which did not cease despite the fact that I had com-menced an attack on the enemy, and shells were continually bursting very close to my aircraft.' Later there would be stern reprimands for the offending anti-aircraft batteries.

As the raiders headed for their impromptu bomb release points, there was some jockeying for position as formations got in each other's way. Kirsch continued: 'Suddenly the Staffel leader called "Don't release, there's a formation of He 111s below!" The He 111 formation slid obliquely under us and was clear. Then came the call "Bombs gone!" Immediately after release we turned, to get out of the danger zone as quickly as possible.'

WEST HAM, 2.45 P.M. When the cannonade began, thirteen-year-old Dan Driscoll and three young friends were walking briskly along Devas Street making for their homes in Canning Town, having been to the Sunday outdoor market at Club Row. The boys heard an almost continual metallic clinking sound, as

The Intended Targets, and the Area of West Ham that was Bombed during the Mid-Afternoon Attack.

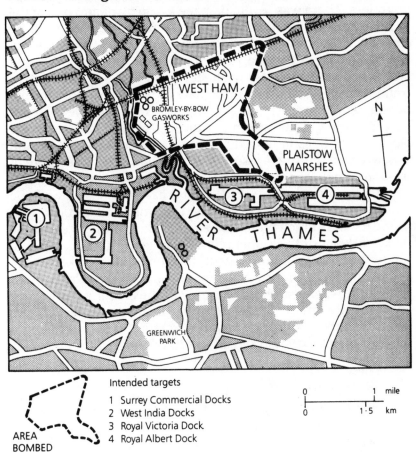

Intended targets

1 Surrey Commercial Docks
2 West India Docks
3 Royal Victoria Dock
4 Royal Albert Dock

AREA BOMBED

shell splinters raining from above bounced off buildings and roads. 'There was a terrific gun barrage, and we were dodging in and out of shop doorways to keep out of the way of the pieces of shrapnel coming down,' Driscoll recalled. Worried more about their parents' reaction if they were late for lunch than anything else, the boys continued on their way.

Then the bombs started exploding across West Ham. Most of the destruction was within an area about three square miles in extent, bounded on the north by the overground railway track for the District Line, on the west by the river Lea, on the east by Plaistow Marshes and on the south by the Royal Victoria Dock.

The Bromley-by-Bow gas works was singled out by the Heinkels of Bomber Geschwader 26, and deluged in a torrent of high-explosive bombs that included five super-heavy 2,200-pounders. There was severe damage to the plant and one of the gas holders was demolished. A bomb fell beside the recently completed St Mary's Hospital, lifting one end of the building and hurling from their bases the boilers for the central heating system. A watchman taking shelter was killed but the incident could have been far worse – the next room, a dormitory for the nursing staff, happened to be empty at the time. Near Upton Park station a train was hit, causing twenty casualties and blocking the lines in both directions. An electricity sub-station was wrecked, cutting off supplies to a wide area. Elsewhere in the borough there was severe damage in residential areas.

With the members of ARP teams assembled at Star Lane school, Irene Cannon sat huddled against a classroom wall trying to get as much protection as possible. For the moment the ARP workers' duty was merely to stay alive, and be ready to render assistance to those outside as soon as the attack ended.

Walking briskly through the empty streets, Dan Driscoll and his friends were nearly home. But with the banging of the guns and their attempts to dodge the falling shell fragments, the boys failed to notice the more potent dangers. 'There was such a racket from the exploding shells, we didn't notice the bombs,' he explained.

SOUTH LONDON, 2.50 P.M. The Dorniers of Bomber Geschwader 2, forming the left-hand column of the raiding force, also arrived over the capital to find that cloud had parted them from their plan. Unable to locate their briefed target, the

Surrey Commercial Docks, the two formations turned through a semi-circle and headed for home without dropping their bombs.

For pilots of the three squadrons of Hurricanes engaging this part of the raiding force, the U-turn was a sudden and unexpected delight. Several were convinced that their presence had scared the German crews into turning away from the capital, and would afterwards say so in their combat reports. In fact both formations of Dorniers had reached the capital intact, having lost only one aircraft on the way in, and would have fought their way to the briefed target had they been able to find it.

On the south-east outskirts of the capital there were few worth-while targets clear of cloud, and on their way out the Dorniers scattered their bombs over several districts. There were reports of damage in Penge, Bexley, Crayford, Dartford and Orpington, but few casualties. The only damage of military significance was at Penge East station, where bombs hit both platforms and blocked the mouth of a tunnel carrying the track to central London.

AT THE SAME TIME as the raiders were turning away from London, those bombers that had become detached from their formations picked through the cloudbanks over Kent playing a deadly game of hide-and-seek with the defenders.

Flying his Dornier on one engine, Werner Kittmann was heading east trying to keep out of everyone's way. 'In cloud we were safe from the fighters. We thought we would be able to sneak home. But as we continued south-east we entered a clear patch of sky. We were at about 2,000 metres. Then flak began detonating behind us, and the bursts got closer and closer.'

Gunner Frank McMachan of No. 166 Battery, Royal Artillery, was manning a Lewis machine gun at the Fort Borstal anti-aircraft gun site at Chatham when the Dornier came past. The plane was beyond range of his own weapon, but he had a grandstand view as the 4.5-in. guns engaged it. 'The bomber was coming from the north-west, heading straight towards our site. Initially we were a bit worried, we thought he might still have his bombs. The guns opened up and I saw the shells detonating around him with black bursts. They were so close I could see the aircraft rocking.' Four sites to the south and east of Chatham, with twelve 4.5-in. and four 3.7-in. guns, reported engaging the lone bomber.

In the cockpit of the Dornier pandemonium reigned. 'Suddenly the pilot called "I can't hold it any longer!"' Kiltmann recalled. 'The elevators were not working. I shouted "Get out!" Then the flight engineer bellowed "Herr Leutnant, my parachute pack has come open." In trying to clip it on either he had picked up the pack by the ripcord, or the ripcord had caught on something. I told him to hold the parachute in his arms against his body. He did so standing on the escape hatch, so I pulled the lever to jettison it. Away it went, with him as well.' The rest of the crew followed as rapidly as they were able.

Frank McMachan watched the Dornier fall out of the sky. 'He started to dive towards the ground, swinging left over Borstal, and the parachutes fell clear. It disappeared amongst houses in Chatham and a cloud of smoke rose from where it hit the ground.'

When the plane crashed, seventeen-year-old shop assistant Gwen Jenkins was making her way to the shelter in the back garden of her home in The Chase, Chatham.

> Suddenly there was an almighty great bang. I knew immediately an aircraft had come down, there were pieces of shiny metal all over the place. The plane had smashed through the top of a house about 100 yards away, the back of the house was ripped off and wreckage was scattered over the gardens and allotments behind it. I was so shaken, I just stood rooted to the spot. The next thing I knew, my dad, of whom I thought the world, was leaping over the waist-high fences one after the other to go and help. I wondered if I would ever see him again. Then the reaction began to set in and I began to shake.

The wreckage had fallen across two Anderson shelters and ten of the occupants were injured, two seriously.

Twenty-four-year-old housewife Florence Tappenden, on a visit to her mother-in-law at Chatham Hill, had been eating Sunday lunch beside the air-raid shelter in the garden. From her vantage point she overlooked most of the town, and had watched Kittmann's bomber being engaged by the anti-aircraft guns and go down. Then her pleasure turned to horror, as she suddenly realized that the ascending cloud of black smoke seemed to be coming from her home. In tears, she dropped everything and ran. But home was two miles away and a woman wearing Sunday best was not dressed for speed; it would take her more than twenty minutes to reach the scene of the crash.

All four crewmen from the German bomber, including the flight engineer whose parachute had opened in the plane, landed safely in or near the town. Kittmann himself came down in someone's back garden between a couple of apple trees. Sitting on the ground releasing his parachute, he looked up to see a civilian standing over him with a shotgun. 'He was elderly and very nervous. He pointed the gun at me, I thought he was about to shoot me. He asked if I was German. I knew little English but I could understand what he meant, and replied "Yes". Then, thank God, three or four soldiers came running over and took me prisoner.'

In another Dornier heading for home on one engine, Herburt Michaelis emerged from cloud and was immediately spotted by Squadron Leader John Sample of No. 504 Squadron. The Hurricane pilot later wrote:

> I started to chase one Dornier which was flying through the tops of clouds. Did you ever see that film *Hell's Angels*? You remember how the Zeppelin came so slowly out of the cloud. Well, this Dornier reminded me of that. I attacked him four times altogether. When he first appeared through the cloud – you know how clouds go up and down like foam on water – I fired at him from the left, swung over to the right, turned in towards another hollow in the cloud where I expected him to reappear, and fired at him again.

One of Sample's attacks shattered the bomber's glass nose, and a round passed through Michaelis's life jacket tearing away the pouch containing the yellow dye marker (to mark his position if he came down in the sea). The fine dust flew everywhere and some went into the German pilot's eyes, blinding him temporarily. Michaelis ordered his crew to bail out, groped his way to the escape hatch and followed. The bomber crashed near Dartford.

At this time Peter Schierning also hoped to get back to France, after one engine of his Heinkel had been wrecked by a flak burst. 'By the engine, part of the skin of the wing had been blown away and I could see the structure inside. I remember thinking what a marvellous aircraft the Heinkel was, being able to stay airborne with that sort of damage.' Then, abruptly, the cloud ran out and the bomber found itself in a clear patch of sky. Almost at once it came under attack from a couple of Hurricanes and a Spitfire. 'They attacked from the rear and the sides, and I saw their tracers coming past the nose of the Heinkel. Early on the intercom was shot away and I had no idea what was happening in the rear of the aircraft, I had no opportunity to use my nose gun.'

The Spitfire pilot was probably Sub-Lieutenant Blake of No. 19 Squadron, who reported attacking 'a stray He 111 which was already being occupied by other friendly fighters'. The Hurricane pilots were Squadron Leader Banham and Flight Lieutenant W. Smith of No. 229 Squadron; later Smith reported that with his commander he went after a lone Heinkel being attacked by a Spitfire: 'I attacked from dead astern with a six-second burst from 200 yards, closing to 150 yards. I saw bullets entering the fuselage and hitting the mainplane. The port engine was smoking and brown oil from the E/A splashed over my windscreen.' When Smith last saw it, the bomber was diving into cloud.

During the attacks one of the Heinkel's gunners was killed and the radio operator was wounded. Schierning heard the pilot shout that the port engine had also been hit and was losing power, there was a fire in the vicinity of the right engine and he was taking the bomber down for a crash landing. 'I made my way back to my crash-landing position behind the pilots – unstrapped in the nose was no place to be for a crash landing. When I reached the position there was a bang and something behind me exploded, jarring my back. We were under attack from fighters until the moment we touched down.' The Heinkel crash-landed near Staplehurst and slithered to a halt in a cloud of dust. When the burning plane came to a stop the crew scrambled out and ran clear.

Another Heinkel of Schierning's Geschwader, also forced out of formation, came under attack from at least twelve Spitfires and Hurricanes from ten different squadrons. With one crewman dead and three wounded, the German pilot attempted a wheels-down landing on West Malling airfield. Again, John Sample had a share in the demise of this bomber: 'I climbed up again to look for some more trouble and found it in the shape of a Heinkel 111 which was being attacked by three Hurricanes and a couple of Spitfires. I had a few cracks at the thing before it made a perfect landing on an RAF aerodrome. Then the Heinkel's undercarriage collapsed, and the pilot pulled up after skidding fifty yards in a cloud of dust.' The fighters continued their attacks on the bomber until it came to a halt, to the intense annoyance of RAF personnel on the ground. The station diarist afterwards noted: 'One enemy aircraft, an He 111, forced down on the aerodrome. Heavy firing from 8 or 9 Hurricanes and Spitfires made aerodrome unhealthy . . .'

That particular Heinkel would be recorded at least seven times in the day's victory tally of enemy aircraft 'definitely destroyed', twice in that for 'probably destroyed' and twice more in that for enemy planes 'damaged'.

Two more Dorniers and four Heinkels, all 'orphans' forced out of formation by battle damage, were finished off by fighters in similar actions at about this time.

As well as the bombers, there were several German fighters limping for home at this time. Unteroffizier Hermann Streibing of Lehr Geschwader 2 had become embroiled with British fighters near London and the wing of his Messerschmitt 109 was damaged. He broke out of the fight and headed east, but shortly afterwards he came under attack from two more British fighters and his plane took further hits. Streibing dived into cloud and shook off his pursuers, but as he levelled out close to the ground he discovered that his radiator had been hit and was leaking glycol. The engine overheating and liable to seize up at any moment, the pilot decided to bail out. He landed heavily on the roof of a house at Hartlip near Sittingbourne. The parachute caught on a chimney and the concussed man was left dangling against one wall unable to move.

Before the Messerschmitt crashed it passed low over the headquarters of No. 307 Heavy Anti-Aircraft Battery, Royal Artillery. Sergeant Don Mackay later recalled: 'The aircraft was going down at a shallow angle, as if it was coming in to land. As it passed over some trees I saw a white parachute start to open behind it, with a man attached. I thought "This chap will never get away with it, he's far too low!"'

Mackay shouted to one of his men to come with him, and the pair ran four-hundred yards over fields to the point where the plane had come down. When they arrived the smouldering wreckage of the fighter lay scattered over the ground beside Hartlip church. 'When we got to the churchyard the wreckage was ablaze, ammunition was exploding all over the place. I fully expected to find the body of the pilot smashed up in a field, he had bailed out far too low.' A glance around the churchyard revealed no sign of the pilot or his parachute. Then, looking round, Mackay noticed a parachute draped over the roof of the house about hundred yards away. 'The man was just hanging there. His parachute would have been only half open, he must have hit the roof then slid down until his parachute caught on the chimney. I told my colleague to make a back, and with the help of a creeper I was able to climb the wall until I reached a bedroom window, then I pulled myself up further using the parachute lines. The German's head was about level with the eaves of the house. Obviously he was very shaken, he asked me "You Englander?" I replied "Ja".'

Unfamiliar with the quick-release box fitted to a parachute harness, Mackay reached in his pocket for his jack knife, intending to cut through the straps. 'By then a small crowd had gathered. One of the people told me how to release the harness, to turn the buckle then bang it with my fist. I tried that several times without success. Then the German realized what I was trying to do, he had by then come to his senses. He had a go at the buckle, the harness opened and he fell to the ground.' Limping on his injured ankle, Streibing was helped to an army truck that had arrived to take him into captivity.

THE HEINKELS of Bomber Geschwader 26 had suffered least of all from the British fighters. Few of the latter had approached the formation, and of those that did most were driven off by the escorts. The unit had suffered only one loss, and that plane had been straggling behind the formation when the fighters caught it.

Yet for Leutnant Roderich Cescotti, piloting one of the bombers, the day was one he would never forget:

> Few Tommies succeeded in penetrating our fighter escort. I saw a Spitfire dive steeply through our escort, level out and close rapidly on our formation. It opened fire, from ahead and to the right, and its tracers streaked towards us. At that moment an Me 109, that we had not seen before, appeared behind the Spitfire and we saw its rounds striking the Spitfire's tail. But the Tommy continued his attack, coming straight for us, and his rounds slashed into our aircraft. We could not return the fire for fear of hitting the Messerschmitt. I put my left arm across my face to protect it from the plexiglass splinters flying around the cockpit, holding the controls with my right hand. With only the thin plexiglass between us, we were eye-to-eye with the enemy's eight machine guns. At the last moment the Spitfire pulled up

and passed very close over the top of us. Then it rolled on its back, as though out of control, and went down steeply trailing black smoke. Waggling its wings, the Messerschmitt swept past us and curved in for another attack. The action lasted only a few seconds, but it demonstrated the determination and bravery with which the Tommies were fighting over their own country.

The courageous Spitfire pilot was Pilot Officer Arthur Pease of No. 603 Squadron who was shot down at a time and place, and in a manner, consistent with Cescotti's account. Pease was still in the cockpit when his blazing fighter dived into the ground near Maidstone at 3.05 p.m.

Although it collected more than thirty hits, Cescotti's Heinkel suffered no serious damage and was able to hold position in formation.

> Fortunately nobody was hurt, and although both engines had taken hits they continued to run smoothly. Ice-cold air blasted through the holes in the plexiglass. So the navigator, with more bravery than circumspection, opened his parachute pack and cut off pieces of silk which he used to block the holes. It was his first operational sortie and I suppose he thought he ought to do something heroic.

Cescotti's Heinkel was not attacked again, and the navigator did not have cause to regret the misuse of his parachute.

ON THE WAY home the Dorniers of Bomber Geschwader 3 came under fighter attack yet again. Heinz Kirsch recalled: '"Achtung, fighters ahead." Friends or foes? Speeding towards us, they came past on either side: Spitfires and Hurricanes. Where were our Me 109s? Nowhere to be seen. As usual, they had run short of fuel and gone home. The enemy fighters turned round and came after us.' A couple of fighters closed on the Dornier from behind. 'Attack followed attack. Yet more impacts! There were bullet holes all over our trusty Dornier. The right motor began to trail smoke and something bright, a panel, fell away. The engine began to shake and the pilot shut it down. The aircraft swung to the side and went into a dive. Then there was a bang, my gun mounting was hit. Warm blood ran down the left side of my face and I realized that something had struck my head.' Kirsch's wound was not serious. While he was regaining his senses, the pilot dived the plane into cloud.

In another Dornier from the same unit, Horst Schulz had had

an engine knocked out during a fighter attack and he too was on his way home alone. Unteroffizier Herbert Groeger, the plane's radio operator, recalled: 'On the way back several fighters sought us out, but they could not nail us. Despite the fact that we had only one engine, the pilot successfully avoided their attacks and luckily none of our guns jammed.' The only injury was to one of the gunners, who had a thumb shot off. As the fighters exhausted their ammunition they broke away from the bomber, until only one was left. Groeger continued: 'The last English fighter stayed with us. It did not move into an attacking position but sat off our right wing. I held up the first-aid kit to show we had a wounded man on board. The English pilot waved a hand to show that he understood, and flew with us almost to the coast before he turned away.'

WEST HAM, 3.05 P.M. As Dan Driscoll neared Durham Road, his main concern was the reception he would get from his father. That fear was so great that he paid scant attention to the damage inflicted on the area in the most recent attack. The boy arrived home to find his parents in the Anderson shelter in their garden, beside themselves with worry for his safety. On seeing him, the parents' anxiety immediately turned to anger. 'Where the bloody hell have you been?' his father shouted and, without waiting for an answer, went on to deliver a stern monologue cataloguing the punishments the boy could expect if he was out again during an air raid.

With three other civil defence workers, Irene Cannon was sent to investigate a bomb incident reported in Percy Street, a few doors from her home. She reached the scene to find two houses demolished and rubble strewn across Percy Road, Avondale Road and Star Lane. One of her duties was to maintain an up-to-date record of the occupants of each house in her area, and note comings and goings. From her notebook she knew there might be as many as five people trapped under the rubble. She ran back to the headquarters to summon 'the heavy mob', a heavy rescue team, to dig them out. The team duly arrived and began systematically pulling away the wreckage. An old man was brought out dead, then the team found an elderly woman seriously injured; one by one the rest of the occupants were brought out, all with shock, cuts and bruises. The dead man was taken by van to the municipal baths at Romford Road, which had been impressed into use as a temporary mortuary. The seriously injured woman went by ambulance to St Mary's Hospital. Those with lesser injuries were escorted on foot to the ARP reception centre at the Star Lane school for tea, sympathy, and an allocation of accommodation if they had nowhere else to go.

As further reports reached the civil defence centres, the extent of the damage and casualties in the area gradually emerged. The worst single incident was at Upland Road where a bomb had exploded beside an Anderson shelter containing six members of the same family; four were killed instantly, one suffered fatal injuries and the other had serious injuries. In Edinburgh Road a high-explosive bomb demolished two houses, killing five people. The diary compiled at the West Ham Main Control Centre recorded sixty-two separate incidents of damage or casualties, of which a few are reproduced below:

Harrold Rd, corner of Green St and Queen's Rd. HE [high-explosive bomb]. Casualties 6, 2 trapped. Green St Blocked. 2 shops demolished. Services sent.

London Rd near Upper Rd. HE. Road blocked. 4 houses demolished. High St by Atlas Rd. HE. Road blocked. LPTB [tram car] cables down. 3 houses demolished.

Conway St and Phillip St. HE. Road blocked. 5 craters. 7 houses demolished.

Unexploded bomb Harold Rd between Green Street and Raymond Rd. Police notified.

Sewer bank cut [between] Upper Rd and Balaam St.

Queens Rd, nr Watson St and May Rd. HE. 5 casualties. 1 crater. Several houses demolished.

Glasgow Rd, between Tweedmouth and Richmond Road. HE. 12 casualties.

West Ham borough records state that 17 people were killed or died of injuries resulting from the attack, 92 were seriously injured and 40 slightly injured.

A few bombs spilled over into the neighbouring borough of East Ham, and the Grangewood telephone exchange was put out of action.

TUNBRIDGE WELLS AREA, 3.10 P.M. With scores of British fighters nipping at their heels, the German formations withdrew in as good order as they were able, assisted by the powerful tail wind. Although it came under severe pressure and there were some gaps in the cover, by and large the German escort plan had held up. Over the middle of Kent the withdrawal covering force swung into position around the bombers: some fifty fresh Messerschmitt 109s with plenty of fuel and magazines full of ammunition.

During this phase the last three British fighter units went into action: Nos 238, 602 and 609 squadrons, with thirty-seven Spitfires and Hurricanes. The Hurricanes of No. 238 Squadron engaged first, going for the Heinkels of Bomber Geschwader 53 and their escorts. Then the two Spitfire squadrons attacked the Dorniers of Bomber Geschwader 2 and shot down two as the raiders were leaving the coast.

Flight Lieutenant George Powell-Sheddon of No. 242 Squadron also took part in this action, and shot down a Dornier 17. After seeing the bomber fall away with its starboard engine trailing smoke, the Hurricane pilot headed north for Duxford in a slow descent to economize on fuel. He made the cardinal error of thinking that because he had had enough of the fighting, his enemy had too. 'I was out of ammunition and tired, and a bit lazy. I was flying home straight and level, it was damn' carelessness on my part.' Seemingly from nowhere a Messerschmitt 109 appeared behind him, his plane shuddered under the impact of hits and started to fall out of control. Powell-Sheddon bailed out and landed with a dislocated shoulder.

Once the bombers were clear of the coast most of the fighting came to an end: Royal Air Force pilots had orders not to pursue the enemy beyond gliding distance from the English coast, for anyone forced down in the English Channel the chances of rescue were poor. A Spitfire of No. 19 Squadron appears to have ignored this injunction, however. It went out over the sea and was shot down by Messerschmitts off the French coast. The pilot was picked up by the German rescue service and taken prisoner.

UXBRIDGE, 3.25 P.M. On the 'tote board' on the wall of Park's operations room, illuminated panels indicated that several squadrons were now 'Landed and Refuelling'. The rest of his squadrons were 'Detailed to Raid' or 'Ordered to Land', indicating that his Group's fighting strength was at its lowest ebb should the enemy decide to launch a follow-up attack. Then

No. 213 Squadron at Tangmere reported that it was again ready for action, its Hurricanes refuelled and rearmed. At Uxbridge the squadron's 'At Readiness' panel illuminated, informing Park and the Prime Minister that the Group again had a fighting reserve, albeit a slender one. For both men it was a moment of profound satisfaction: the RAF commander had thrown into action every Spitfire and Hurricane he had, and the gamble had paid off. During the minutes that followed, other squadrons' 'At Readiness' panels lit up. No. 11 Group's crisis was over.

Despite the extensive cloud cover and the delay in scrambling the 'Big Wing', in general the fighter controllers performed their task in exemplary fashion. During the noon action, it will be remembered, twenty-three squadrons of fighters had been scrambled and all except one made contact with the enemy. During the afternoon action twenty-eight squadrons of Spitfires and Hurricanes had been scrambled and every one of them went into action.

CHATHAM, 3.25 P.M. Florence Tappenden reached her home in The Chase, breathless and tearful after the run from her mother-in-law's. She found that the German plane had crashed not on her house but a neighbour's. Police had cordoned off the area, and she was let in only after she could prove that she lived there. Blazing wreckage had spilled across her garden, but otherwise her home was undamaged.

The crash site was a magnet for small boys living nearby, and ten-year-old Eric Sutton was one of several who came trotting to the scene. 'When we got to The Chase we saw the bomber's tail sticking out of the roof of a house. The rest of the plane was scattered across about three gardens. The wreckage was burning itself out. I was able to get a piece of the nose as a souvenir.'

KILNDOWN, 3.25 P.M. War brings danger in many forms, and the small boys' unthinking quest for pieces of crashed enemy planes sometimes ended in tragedy. The Dornier that Paddy Stephenson had rammed plunged into an orchard near Kildown and caught fire. The wreckage was still burning about an hour later when one of the bombs suddenly 'cooked off'. At the time of the explosion several would-be souvenir hunters were waiting for the flames to die down before moving in on the prize, three were killed and nine injured.

STRAIT OF DOVER, 3.30 P.M. As during the noon action, despite the losses suffered, the bomber formations held together while over England. As each crossed the south coast, it wheeled on to a heading for its base airfield. Aircraft with wounded on board, or those with severe damage, pulled away to land at the first possible opportunity after crossing the French coast. Meanwhile, the Messerschmitts of the withdrawal covering force left their charges and headed back over southern England, anxiously searching for damaged aircraft and stragglers to shepherd clear of enemy territory.

Probably the first German bomber to put down on friendly territory was the badly shot-up Dornier carrying Heinz Kirsch. It made a crash landing on sand dunes near Dunkirk.

Horst Schulz took his Dornier back to Antwerp on one engine, and made a wheels-down landing on a meadow with both main wheels locked and the tyres cut to ribbons.

> As the Dornier touched down it stood on its nose, and slid along the ground on the nose and the two main wheels. When the plane came to a halt, the tail dropped to the ground with a crash. We were home!
>
> The radio operator lowered the entry hatch and a stream of spent cartridge cases clattered on the grass. Carefully we lowered the wounded flight engineer to the ground and carried him about twenty metres clear of the plane. Then we lit cigarettes – that was one of the most enjoyable I ever smoked!
>
> At first there was nobody around, then some civilians appeared and finally some German soldiers arrived and summoned an ambulance. With the radio operator I walked round the aircraft to inspect the damage, stroking the trusty Dornier that had brought us home. There were more than two hundred bullet holes. I peeped inside the cowling of the starboard engine to see what was wrong with it. An entire cylinder head had been shot away and was lying in the bottom of the cowling.

DURING THE hard-fought action that afternoon, the Luftwaffe lost 21 bombers and at least 12 fighters. The Royal Air Force lost 15 fighters destroyed and 21 damaged, a serious loss but one it could recover from. The main engagement of the day was over, and nobody on either side could have the slightest doubt that Fighter Command was still in business.

Chapter 5

THE DAY'S OTHER ACTIONS

2.23 p.m. to Midnight

War is a rough, violent trade.

Johann Schiller

VILLACOUBLAY NEAR PARIS, 2.23 P.M. At the same time as
Air Vice-Marshal Park had ordered his last Spitfires and Hurricanes into the air to engage the raiders approaching London,
twenty-seven Heinkels of Bomber Geschwader 55 began taking
off from bases around Paris. Once airborne the bombers assembled into formation. One turned back with mechanical trouble,
the rest headed north-west in a steady climb.

This was the German follow-up attack which Park and the
Prime Minister had feared, but it would not be launched in the
way they expected. Acting on the premise that the Royal Air
Force had concentrated every available fighter for the defence of
London, the Heinkels, without fighter escort, were to attack the
Royal Navy base at Portland.

For Fighter Command the first indication of the new German
thrust came at 3.05 p.m. when the raiders appeared on radar.
Plotted just to the north of Cherbourg, the force was designated
Raid 50 and assessed at '6 plus' aircraft. The formation was
tracked approaching the Dorset coast, but, because of the radar
operators' underestimation of its strength, No. 10 Group's
fighter controllers failed to take the new threat seriously. Thus
the bombers were able to reach Portland at 3.30 p.m. and deliver
their attack without being intercepted. Considering that the
defence at the naval base comprised only a single obsolete 3-in.
anti-aircraft gun, and the skies over the target were clear, the
raid achieved remarkably little. At the naval base there was

Targets on the South Coast attacked by German Bombers during the Afternoon of 15 September.

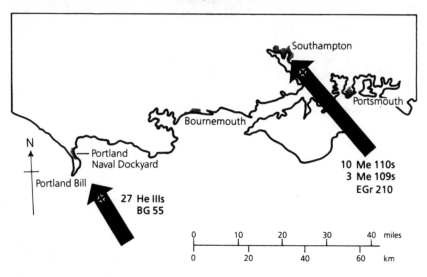

minor damage to buildings, two people were killed and fourteen wounded.

Only as the Heinkels were running in to bomb was a flight of six Spitfires of No. 152 Squadron ordered to intercept the raid. The German planes had completed their attack and turned for home before the fighters caught up with them. Pilot Officer Eric Marrs, leading the flight, was over Weymouth when he sighted the German formation. 'I climbed up to come in behind them from the sun, but they were going faster than I thought. They were in tight formation and they dropped their bombs on Portland Bill from 16,000 feet doing pattern bombing. We then came in on their tails and they turned out to sea. We chased them for about 10 miles, nibbling at the rear end of the formation.'

The Spitfires split into two sections of three, and Pilot Officer O'Brien led his section against a Heinkel straggling some distance behind the formation. The fighters made five separate firing runs on the bomber, inflicting severe damage and setting one of its engines ablaze. The bomber went into a steep dive and crashed into the sea. Only one crew man was rescued.

Marrs led his section in an attack on the Heinkel at the left rear of the formation, then against the bomber on the right rear. Unteroffizier Heinrich Snedel was radio operator and mid-

108

upper gunner in the latter: 'Three fighters singled us out for attack. Two came in from above and the flight engineer and I engaged them with our machine guns. They closed to about 100 metres then broke away; their fire was relatively ineffective. The third fighter attacked us from below, where our defensive armament was weakest. He closed to short range and opened fire, inflicting numerous hits.' Eric Marrs had attacked the bomber from below. His rounds killed one of the German gunners, wounded another and damaged one of the Heinkel's engines.

By the time Marrs had completed his attack the bombers were well out to sea. Rather than become involved in an extended tail-chase towards enemy territory, Marrs ordered the Spitfires to break off the action and return to base. His account continued: 'If we had had the whole squadron up we could have broken up their formation and knocked down quite a number. The extraordinary part about this raid was that there was no fighter escort. I was keeping a very good look-out, though, in case such a thing should suddenly appear out of the sun.'

Suedel's pilot took the damaged Heinkel back across the Channel on one engine, and made a wheels-down landing at an airstrip near Cherbourg.

THE HEINKEL FORMATION faded from the British radar screens at 3.46 p.m., and for over an hour no hostile aircraft was over southern England. Then, at 5.25 p.m., yet another threat appeared on the British plotting tables: Raid 49 assessed at '35 plus' aircraft. In fact this force comprised only thirteen aircraft; as if to compensate for the earlier underestimation, the radar operators overestimated the strength of this one by a factor of three.

The new attack force comprised ten Messerschmitt 110s and three Messerschmitt 109s from Erprobungs Gruppe 210, a specialized fighter-bomber unit. The aircraft all carried bombs and their target was the Supermarine works at Southampton, one of the most important plants assembling Spitfires. This was an attempt to hit Fighter Command where it would hurt most.

The fighter controllers at No. 10 Group headquarters scrambled three squadrons of fighters to meet the threat; those at No. 11 Group scrambled four more. But the fighter-bombers' high-speed approach took the defenders by surprise, and once again the raiders were able to reach their target without being intercepted.

Alexander McKee, 22, an air enthusiast waiting to join the Royal Air Force, was drinking tea at a café in Stoneham, three miles north of the target, when sirens sounded in the area. Afterwards he noted in his diary:

> The siren moaned half-heartedly for an instant. I went outside on hearing enemy planes. I counted them aloud. Ten. They dived straight down on Southampton, without any preliminaries, through the barrage of gunfire, one after the other. Alfred saw a bomb released, then handed the glasses to me.
>
> The aircraft had twin rudders, and might have been Dorniers or Jaguars [a bomber version of the Messerschmitt 110 thought to have been in use by the Luftwaffe at that time]. The dives were fast but shallow, and they pulled out of them at 2,000 feet. It was not a dive-bombing attack proper.
>
> Soldiers passed inane remarks about 'nothing could live in that barrage', although the Germans were very obviously living in it and bombing in it, too. The barrage was quite good, but none of the Huns were brought down . . . Very quickly and efficiently the Germans re-formed and disappeared into a cloud. I have never seen a better bit of flying than those Nazi pilots put up – they got into formation like a well-drilled team, in the teeth of the guns.

McKee's account accurately describes the tactics used by Erpro-bungs Gruppe 210, whose planes attacked individually and released their bombs in 45-degree shallow dives.

Despite their apparently skilful attack, the raiders failed to find their target in the middle of a built-up area and the Super-marine works escaped damage. The main concentration of bombs landed on a residential district a few hundred yards east of the factory, demolishing several houses and damaging others; 9 people were killed, 10 seriously injured and 23 slightly injured. Other bombs fell near the Thornycroft boat yard and the railway track and station at Woolston.

As the fighter-bombers were leaving the target, Hurricanes of No. 607 Squadron intercepted them and claimed two 'Dornier 17s' shot down. The misidentification of Messerschmitt 110s as Dorniers is understandable, but the claim was erroneous: from German records it is clear that Erprobungs Gruppe 210 lost no aircraft on that day.

Later McKee cycled to Woolston to observe the results of the attack. The Supermarine works was untouched, but, he noted in his diary, 'buildings nearby were not what they used to be. Woolston station was surrounded by craters and wrecked houses. Two large bombs had straddled the railway bridge, leaving it untouched except by splinters. Most of the roads around had collected a bomb or two. The Nazi bomb-aiming had been as bad as their flying had been good . . .'

SOME MYSTERY SURROUNDS the loss of a Beaufighter of No. 25 Squadron late that afternoon. The plane crashed near Kenley airfield at 6.20 p.m., killing the crew of three, and it is unclear whether the loss resulted from enemy action or a flying accident. That day Feldwebel Neuhoff of Fighter Geschwader 53 was credited with shooting down a 'Bristol Blenheim'. The Royal Air Force did not lose a Blenheim, but the Beaufighter could easily have been mistaken for one.

THAT EVENING sunset was at 7.12 p.m. During the evening twilight Royal Air Force day fighters went into action one last time, when Flight Lieutenant Ken Gillies leading three Spitfires of No. 66 Squadron was vectored on to a lone German nuisance raider. They intercepted the intruder, a Heinkel 111, at 8,000 feet near Gravesend. Using cloud to approach unseen, Gillies closed to 300 yards behind the raider and fired a four-second burst into it, but had to break off his attack when the Heinkel dived into cloud. Attacking whenever they had an opportunity, the fighters chased the bomber in and out of cloud all the way to the coast. When last seen, their victim was heading south over the sea with its port engine stopped. Gillies afterwards reported: 'I ran out of ammunition so proceeded to shadow EA and reported his track to Control. Finally EA disappeared in cloud over coast 10 miles E of Dungeness. Before losing sight of him I flew close and observed rear gunner was out of action and considerable damage to fuselage.'

From German records it is clear that the Heinkel belonged to Bomber Geschwader 1. Badly shot up, it crash-landed near St Valery-sur-Somme with three wounded crewmen. The plane was damaged beyond repair.

BY 8 P.M. darkness had fallen over southern England, and soon afterwards London's sirens sounded to warn of the approach of the first of the night's raiders, seven Junkers 88s of Bomber Gruppe 806.

This time there was moderate cloud cover over the capital, and the same bright harvest moon as on the previous night. During the four hours to midnight a further seventy-seven bombers, Junkers 88s and Heinkel 111s of Air Fleet 3, ran in to drop their loads on London.

Up to midnight several serious incidents were reported in the capital. A bomb fell on St Thomas's Hospital and started a major conflagration; 3 people were killed, 10 seriously injured and 30 had minor injuries. Guy's Hospital was hit by two bombs, one of which failed to explode; all operating theatres and the main casualty department had to be evacuated until the bomb was made safe. Lambeth Hospital also suffered damage. In Bermondsey a bomb struck the town hall, trapping twenty people sheltering in the basement until rescue workers could free them.

German bombs were not the only hazard facing Londoners that night. Of the anti-aircraft shells fired, a small proportion failed to detonate in the sky and fell to the ground intact. Any that landed on a hard surface was liable to go off on impact. One such shell fell on the Isolation Hospital at Winchmore Hill and exploded, killing two people and injuring two more.

Also on the night of the 15th, nine Heinkels of Bomber Geschwader 27 bombed Liverpool. This attack opened at 10.48 p.m. and was still in progress at midnight. Widespread damage was reported in the city and in neighbouring Birkenhead, but there were only nine casualties.

Elsewhere in the country bomb damage was reported at Eastbourne, Worthing, Bournemouth, Cardiff, Avonmouth, Manchester, Warrington, Bootle and Preston.

During the night of the 15th/16th, Fighter Command Blenheims, Beaufighters, Defiants and Hurricanes flew sixty-four sorties. By midnight two night fighters reported that they had intercepted enemy bombers, but no victories were claimed by fighters or the anti-aircraft guns.

AFTER DARK ON THE 15th, Royal Air Force bombers were also busy. More than 150 Battles, Blenheims, Hampdens, Wellingtons and Whitleys took off to attack the channel ports, and Krefeld, Soest, Hamburg, Wilhelmshaven, Cuxhaven and other targets in Germany. Two of the four Whitleys dispatched against Berlin reported attacking the city.

Although the raiders reported causing damage to all their targets, German records indicate that the attacks were a good deal less effective than the participants thought. The only serious damage was at Antwerp, where an ammunition dump was set off, and at Calais where fire destroyed the main railway station. In Germany the worst single incident was at Krefeld, where a residential area was hit and two people killed and seven injured.

All the Royal Air Force bombers would return to their bases, though one had serious damage. When midnight struck, a Hampden of No. 83 Squadron was heading over the North Sea to bomb the port of Antwerp. In the course of its attack the plane would be hit by flak and set on fire. The wireless operator, 18-year-old Sergeant John Hannah, would fight the flames and extinguish them, though in the process he would suffer serious burns. For bravery beyond the call of duty, John Hannah would later receive the Victoria Cross.

Also that night, six Swordfish aircraft of the Fleet Air Arm laid mines in the estuary of the river Schelde and off Flushing.

So ended 15 September 1940, a day that ended German hopes of victory in the Battle of Britain. Before considering the implications of those events and their effect on the course of the war, let us examine the day's events as a whole and then see how the media presented them to the public in Great Britain and Germany.

Chapter 6

15 SEPTEMBER 1940: AN OVERVIEW

What has not been examined impartially has not been well examined. Scepticism is therefore the first step toward truth.

Denis Diderot

IN THE TWENTY-FOUR HOURS under review, the Luftwaffe flew about 1,261 sorties over England: 437 by bombers, 769 by single-engined fighters, about 40 by twin-engined fighters and about 15 by reconnaissance aircraft. Of the sorties, 219 were flown during the nights of the 14th/15th and 15th/16th; the remaining sorties, just over 1,000, were flown during the daylight hours of the 15th.

In the course of its operations against England the Luftwaffe lost 56 aircraft, all during the daylight hours. This loss represented 5.5 per cent of the force committed. Thirty-five of the German planes lost, nearly two-thirds of the total, came down in England; the other 21 crashed in the sea. Three German planes returned damaged beyond repair; 23 others had lesser damage. In the course of the action the Luftwaffe lost 81 aircrew killed or missing, 63 taken prisoner and 31 wounded.

The bombers were the main targets for the British fighters. In the noon action, of twenty-five Dornier 17s of Bomber Geschwader 76 that attacked London, six (24 per cent) were shot down. Strong headwinds and other problems had delayed the bombers' arrival over the capital, resulting in a hiatus in the escort plan. Thus the Dorniers had no fighter cover at the target, as they came under attack from no fewer than eleven squadrons of Spitfires and Hurricanes. As has been said earlier, given the strength of the fighter defences it is remarkable that any

114

of the bombers survived; that nearly three-quarters of the Dorniers regained the coast of France speaks highly for the leadership of Major Alois Lindmayr, the flying skill and discipline of his crews, and the amazing ruggedness of the Dornier 17.

Of the 114 German bombers that crossed the coast of England for the afternoon attack, 21 (18 per cent) were shot down. As is usual in a large-scale air action, losses varied greatly from unit to unit. Hardest-hit was the formation leading the right-hand column of bombers, the 19 Dorniers of Bomber Geschwader 3. That particular formation drew nearly all the fighter attacks made on that column, and it lost 6 aircraft (31 per cent). Thus shielded, the following formation comprising 27 Heinkels of Bomber Geschwader 26 had virtually a clear run to and from the target and lost only one aircraft (4 per cent), the lowest loss rate of all.

The author has no hard evidence that any German aircraft was shot down that day by anti-aircraft guns alone; guns shared at least four victories with fighters, however.

In mounting the attacks on London, the immutable laws of geography placed a tactical strait-jacket round the shoulders of the German planners. Everything was governed by the limited radius of action of the Messerschmitt 109. If the raiding formation took the most direct route and there were no unforeseen hitches, this fighter carried just sufficient fuel to escort the bombers to the target and for the first part of the way home. Then the Me 109s had to break away and go home and a fresh force met the bombers to cover the rest of the withdrawal. Any deviation from the most direct route to the target reduced the time the escorts could remain in position. This author has no criticism of the tactical routing of the German formations attacking London on that day.

The day in question was the only one on which the Luftwaffe launched two separate daylight attacks on London. Each incursion sparked off a large-scale action, so it is to be expected that losses on both sides would be greater than on days when there was only one attack on the capital. Some commentators have criticized the Luftwaffe planners for mounting the double attack. This author does not. The essence of good tactical planning is to ring the changes as often as possible and, as we have observed, the Germans did not have many options available.

The 'right' tactic can become the wrong one if it is employed too often. And a 'wrong' tactic can become the correct one if it takes an enemy by surprise and catches him off balance. The double attack was a reasonable tactical ploy and there was nothing wrong in using it.

The German planners believed, erroneously as it turned out, that Fighter Command would commit all of its fighters to defend London during the two main attacks. Even so, the attack on Portland by a Gruppe of Heinkels without fighter escort was an unnecessary act of bravado. Air Fleet 3 possessed two Gruppen of Messerschmitt 110s which played no part in the day's fighting and which could have provided a useful degree of cover. Fortunately for the Heinkels' crews, the Royal Air Force fighter controllers misread this attack and the defensive response was too little and too late.

FOLLOWING THE COMBATS on 15 September, several German bombers regained their bases with more than a hundred hits from .303-in. rounds fired by British fighters. An important factor assisting the survival of German aircraft was the self-sealing fuel tank developed following lessons learned during the Spanish Civil War. In that conflict the Luftwaffe lost several aircraft after shell fragments or bullets punctured their fuel tanks. Often the loss of fuel prevented the plane regaining friendly territory, or the leaking fuel caught fire and the aircraft's demise was more immediate and spectacular.

The self-sealing fuel tank developed in Germany was made of compressed cellulose fibre, with a self-sealing covering 1 cm. thick comprising alternate layers of vulcanized and non-vulcanized rubber, and an outer covering of leather. If a machine-gun round pierced the tank, the passage of fuel through the hole set up a chemical reaction with the non-vulcanized rubber; the latter swelled and sealed the hole. In the Battle of Britain the new tanks proved very effective against the small-calibre rounds fired by British fighters, and many a German bomber was saved from the fiery end that would otherwise have been its fate.

AFTER THE action on 15 September the defenders claimed the destruction of 185 German aircraft. Close examination of British records reveals the reason for this huge overclaim. Fifteen of the

German planes shot down were claimed more than once, and some were claimed several times. A prime example was the Dornier 17 that crashed beside Victoria station. The only bomber to fall within twenty miles of the centre of London during the noon action, it was separately claimed by no fewer than nine fighter pilots. All of these claims were accepted at face value by the authorities. In the afternoon action, the Heinkel 111 forced to land on West Malling airfield was claimed seven times 'definitely destroyed', twice 'probably destroyed' and twice as 'damaged'.

Neither side had a monopoly on overclaiming, and the German claim of 79 British planes destroyed on that day was proportionally almost as much in error as the British claim.

DURING THE PERIOD under review Royal Air Force Fighter Command flew 797 operational sorties, including 92 on the nights of the 14th/15th and 15th/16th. By this stage of the battle the Luftwaffe intelligence service believed that Fighter Command was at the end of its tether, and the British reaction to the German attacks was vastly stronger than had been expected.

In the hours of daylight Fighter Command flew 705 operational sorties – a number that was, coincidentally, almost equal to the number of serviceable Spitfires and Hurricanes in its order of battle. That was two-thirds the total number of sorties flown by the Luftwaffe for all types of aircraft, but it was *nine-tenths* the number of sorties flown by the German single-engined fighters. The 705 daylight sorties by Fighter Command can be divided into the following categories:

	Patrols	Fighters
To intercept enemy aircraft	78	604
Convoy protection	3	8
Sector patrols	33	92
Other	1	1

Intercept sorties were those where fighters were scrambled to engage hostile aircraft tracked on radar or by the ground observer posts. Convoy protection patrols were standing patrols over shipping likely to come under air attack. Sector patrols were standing patrols sent up to meet no specific threat; these fighters were often vectored to intercept high-flying reconnaissance aircraft or nuisance raiders that could not be caught by fighters scrambled from the ground. The 'other' category embraced the single Spitfire sortie by Alan Wright to observe the approach of the German raiding force in the afternoon action and report on its composition.

Of the 604 interception sorties a total of 417 (69 per cent) made contact with the enemy. In the two large-scale actions to defend London, however, the proportion of fighters engaging the enemy was far higher than the overall figure suggests. On that day Air Chief Marshal Dowding's fighter control system functioned at its triumphant best. In the morning twenty-three squadrons of Spitfires and Hurricanes were scrambled and twenty-two engaged. In the afternoon twenty-eight squadrons were scrambled, all of them engaged.

During the main afternoon action all except two of the Category A Squadrons, Nos 56 and 152 in No. 10 Group, were committed. No Category B squadrons engaged but two Category C units took part – Nos 302 and 611 Squadrons which came south with the No. 12 Group Big Wing.

In contesting the smaller raids on coastal targets, the fighter control system worked less well. In the case of the attack on Portland, the controllers misread the German intentions completely. Only one half-squadron was dispatched to intercept the bombers, and it engaged only after the attack was over. Five squadrons of fighters were scrambled to intercept the attack by fighter-bombers on Southampton; of these only one squadron engaged, and that too was as the raiders were leaving the target.

THAT AFTERNOON, for a period of nearly an hour, every Spitfire and Hurricane squadron based on the south-east of England was committed. Some writers have suggested that Fighter Command as a whole was at full stretch at this time, but this was not so. When Air Vice-Marshal Park told the Prime Minister that he had no reserves, he was referring only to No. 11 Group and the adjacent sectors. In fact, at that time, less than half of Fighter Command's available Spitfires and Hurricanes had been committed; the remainder, belonging to Nos 10, 12 and 13 Groups, sat out the action at bases in the west and north of the country. Even if the Luftwaffe had inflicted the hoped-for heavy losses on Figher Command, within twenty-four hours the hardest-hit units would have been replenished with aircraft and pilots.

In the two main actions 192 Spitfire sorties (37 per cent of the total) and 327 Hurricane sorties (63 per cent) engaged the enemy. On average, one German aircraft was destroyed for every nine Spitfires or Hurricanes that went into action.

Eight Spitfires and twenty Hurricanes were destroyed in air combat, all of them in the large-scale actions in front of London. Thirteen of the British fighters fell to attacks by enemy fighters, six to return fire from the bombers and nine to unknown causes. The eight Spitfires lost represented just over 4 per cent of the sorties they flew, and the twenty Hurricanes lost represented just over 6 per cent of the sorties they flew. Because of its superior performance, a Spitfire making contact with the enemy was two-thirds less likely to be shot down than a Hurricane. A large proportion of the German aircraft destroyed were engaged more than once, and it is not possible to draw meaningful conclusions on the relative effectiveness of the Spitfire and the Hurricane as destroyers of enemy planes.

Twelve Royal Air Force pilots were killed or died of wounds immediately following the action, a further twelve were wounded, and one was taken prisoner. Thus it cost the Luftwaffe seven aircrew killed, missing, wounded or taken prisoner for each pilot casualty inflicted on the Royal Air Force. Historians have made much of the erosion of Fighter Command's strength during the Battle of Britain, but even as a proportion of the total force the German aircrew losses were significantly higher.

In the course of the air fighting that day there were four mid-air collisions, three deliberate and one accidental. Mid-air collisions were not uncommon during close-fought combats involving large numbers of aircraft, but it was unusual to have so many in so short a period. All eight aircraft involved in the collisions were wrecked, and they amounted to nearly 10 per cent of the total number of planes destroyed.

THE GERMAN BOMBERS' intended objectives, the concentration of railway lines in west London and the dock areas in the east, were all justifiable military targets. So was the Bromley-by-Bow gasworks bombed as a secondary target that afternoon. But any attack on targets close to residential areas was bound to

119

cause civilian casualties. In the Greater London area 57 civilians were killed, 87 seriously injured and 66 slightly injured. Civilian casualties in the rest of the country were 10 killed, 32 seriously injured and 31 slightly injured.

THE WEATHER obstructed both the German attacks on London. In each case the powerful headwind slowed the approach of the raiders, allowing the defenders more time to concentrate forces to meet the raids. In the late morning these winds were an important contributory factor in forcing the escorting Messerschmitt 109s to run short of fuel and break off the action before reaching the capital.

London was covered in between seven- and nine-tenths cloud cover when the German bombers attacked. At noon the sky happened to be clear over Battersea, allowing the bombers to deliver an accurate attack. In the afternoon action all the bombers' primary targets were blanketed by cloud, causing the raiders to deposit their bombs over a wide area and to little military effect.

THE POPULAR VIEW of the Battle of Britain, as depicted in post-war films, is of a series of large-scale, close-fought dogfights between the opposing fighters, and of fighters weaving in and out of bomber formations carrying out attack after attack. These impressions are misleading. If escorting Messerschmitts were in the area – as was usually the case – Spitfire or Hurricane pilots were usually forced to make high-speed slashing attacks on the enemy bomber formations. They would close on their prey as rapidly as possible, fire one or more short bursts, then dive away. Any Royal Air Force pilot who slowed down for fancy manoeuvring in the vicinity of a bomber formation risked coming under a vicious cross-fire from his intended victims. He also left himself vulnerable to Messerschmitts diving from above.

Very few one-to-one manoeuvring combats between fighters lasted more than twenty seconds. Any pilot who concentrated his attention for too long on one enemy fighter risked surprise attack from another. As has been said, during the research for this book the author has found *only one* recorded instance of a protracted combat involving a single fighter from each side on this day: during the afternoon, between a Messerschmitt 109 and the Spitfire flown by Squadron Leader Lane of No. 19 Squadron. The combat appears to have ended inconclusively.

ANALYSIS OF the day's actions casts new light on the effectiveness of Douglas Bader's 'Big Wing' tactics. In the course of the Battle of Britain the five-squadron Big Wing made contact with large forces of enemy aircraft on only three occasions: twice on 15 September and once on the 18th. The intention was that the two squadrons of Spitfires would fend off the German escorts while the three squadrons of Hurricanes delivered a concerted attack on the bombers.

At noon the Big Wing met the enemy on the most favourable terms imaginable: its 56 fighters pounced on a formation of 25 Dorniers, without escorts, over the centre of London. Initially the Wing had to hold back while fighters of No. 11 Group completed their attacks. Then the five squadrons attacked in turn and there were several instances of Spitfires and Hurricanes crowding each other out in their attempts to get at the bombers.

Any combat involving a large number of aircraft will give rise to heavy overclaiming and, by definition, any engagement in which the Big Wing took part involved a large number of aircraft. In the noon action the Big Wing claimed 26 German aircraft destroyed, including 20 bombers, for no loss to itself. Fighters from the Big Wing shared in the destruction of 5, possibly all 6, of the Dorniers actually shot down during the action, claiming most of them several times.

In the afternoon the Big Wing was itself pounced on by German fighters, and broken up before it could get close to the bombers. There was much confusion and at least one near-collision (as Bader himself described). The Wing split into small units, some of which attacked the bombers, and their pilots claimed the destruction of 26 enemy aircraft including 17 bombers (in total 21 bombers were brought down during that action).

Both Big Wing actions on September 15 were characterized by considerable overclaiming. During the war, and for many years after it, this overclaiming would lead to an exaggerated assessment of the effectiveness of the Big Wing tactics. With hindsight it is clear that the five-squadron Wing was too large and unwieldy for one man to direct effectively in combat. In terms of enemy aircraft destroyed, the Big Wing was rather less effective

121

than an equivalent number of squadrons going into action in ones and twos.

These negative aspects of the Big Wing operations were more than counter-balanced, however, by the one aspect in which they were unfailingly and resoundingly successful: the devastating effect they had on German morale. Before the action on 15 September, Luftwaffe crews had been told that they would face only the remnant of an almost-defeated British fighter force. The approach flight across Kent, in which the bombers came under repeated attack from fresh squadrons of Spitfires and Hurricanes, cast doubts on the accuracy of that intelligence. Then to arrive at the outskirts of London and be confronted by more than fifty Royal Air Force fighters approaching in parade-formation, that caused an implosion of confidence on the German side.

One hundred and forty years earlier Napoleon Bonaparte had commented: 'In war, the morale is to the material as three is to one.' Each time it went into action, the Big Wing demonstrated beyond possible doubt that the Royal Air Force was far from beaten. If the new tactics did nothing else but impress that unpalatable fact on the Luftwaffe, they were well worth the effort involved.

Chapter 7

MEDIA ASSESSMENTS

How clear, convincing, eloquent and bold
The barefaced lie, with manly vigour told.

Lord Canning

HAVING EXAMINED the events of 15 September 1940, let us observe how accurately they were portrayed in British and German newspapers at the time.

In its issue for 16 September, *The Times* described the previous day's air action in the following terms:

175 RAIDERS SHOT DOWN
Sunday Air Battles Over London and S.E.
Third Attack on Buckingham Palace
RAF Batter Invasion Machine

The RAF inflicted on the German Air Force yesterday one of the most severe defeats it has yet suffered. In fierce fighting which resulted from persistent attacks on London and South-East England, 175 Enemy machines were destroyed. Thirty British Fighters were lost, but 10 of the pilots are safe.

For the third time within a week Buckingham Palace was bombed during an air raid on London yesterday morning. The Queen's private apartments were damaged and small fires, which were soon put out, were started in the grounds. Their Majesties were not in the Palace at the time.

Among the places in London where enemy machines crashed yesterday were Kennington Oval, Streatham and Victoria. During the week-end the RAF continued their devastating raids against the enemy's invasion machine. Many Channel and North Sea ports were bombed, the havoc being particularly severe at Antwerp. Railways junctions in Western Germany were also badly damaged.

The mention of enemy aircraft crashing at 'Kennington Oval, Streatham and Victoria' was true only in the case of the last of these. The Kennington Oval report stemmed from the fact that a German airman landed there by parachute, having bailed out of the bomber that crashed beside Victoria station. The Streatham incident stemmed from a gas main ignited by a German bomb. The report in *The Times* continued:

> The official communiqué stated that during the day between 350 and 400 enemy aircraft had launched attacks on the capital in two waves, with an estimated 200 fighters and bombers in each.
>
> In every case fighter patrols were ready to meet the enemy. The two main attacks on the London area received such a gruelling as never before. Spitfire and Hurricane squadrons, many of them veterans in London defence, fought them over the Kent coast as they came in, fought them over Maidstone and Canterbury above the Medway and Thames Estuary. Many were turned away. The survivors they fought again over London itself, squadron after squadron of fighters flying fresh into action. Finally they chased them back again and out over the Channel whence they came.

The author has found no evidence of any German formation being 'turned away' by British fighters. However, during the afternoon attack the Dorniers of Bomber Geschwader 2 arrived over London to find their assigned targets covered by cloud. The two formations turned away without bombing, and were seen to do so by defending pilots who afterwards reported the fact.

The newspapers eagerly seized on the reports of damage to Buckingham Palace as evidence of a deliberate German plan to harm the British Royal Family. *The Times* reported:

> The attack on Buckingham Palace yesterday occurred during the first of the daylight raids, the warning for which in London was sounded shortly after noon.
>
> Two heavy bombs fell, one on the Palace buildings and one on the lawn. Neither of them exploded, but one of them damaged the Queen's private apartments.
>
> A number of small incendiary bombs fell at the same time in the Palace grounds, and some of them started small fires on the grass. These were quickly got under control by the Palace ARP and the police.
>
> The King and Queen were not in residence at the Palace at the time, and only a skeleton staff of servants and others was on duty. All were in the basement shelters, and there were no casualties.

The bomb which struck the Palace building crashed through the tapestry room on the first floor, which was used by the Queen as a drawing room. It tore a hole in the ceiling.

Onlookers stated that they saw the German aeroplane high over the Palace and heard the whistle of bombs. Then they saw British fighters attacking the raider.

A few seconds later a German aeroplane was seen to break in pieces, the wings went fluttering in one direction while the fuselage fell like a stone.

In fact, as we have seen, the 'attack on Buckingham Palace' was caused by two small 110-pound bombs and a canister of incendiaries that tore from the Dornier tumbling out of the sky after Ray Holmes rammed it.

By Tuesday the 17th, the British victory claim for the previous Sunday had risen to 185 aircraft: 178 by fighters and 7 by anti-aircraft guns. These figures were reported in the press, backed by assurances on the scrupulous care taken in compiling the victory total. A *Times* editorial on the 17th stated:

Complete reports issued yesterday show that Sunday's attacks on this country cost the German Air Force more machines and more men than it has ever lost before in a single day. The figures were 185 aircraft and at least 450 airmen, and they are compiled on the strict principle laid down by the Air Ministry that crippled machines which stagger home, often with some of their crews killed or wounded, are not counted.

As mentioned in the previous chapter, the figure of 185 German aircraft destroyed was the total of claims reported by individual fighter pilots and anti-aircraft gun units following each phase of the action. These numbers were not inflated for propaganda purposes. There was no need to, since the figures were good enough as they stood.

No serious attempt was made to correlate the available evidence on the day's claims, until the publication of captured German records after the war. Compared with the actual German loss of 56 aircraft destroyed during the attacks on Great Britain, the original British figure was a three-fold overclaim.

Initial Royal Air Force press releases stated that 30 British fighters had been lost during the action. Later that figure was reduced to 25. The true figure was 29. The report of 12 Royal Air Force pilots killed in the action was accurate.

One further British loss in combat that day was admitted in a separate communiqué: the Whitley bomber which failed to return from the attack on the invasion ports.

IN GERMANY, official communiqués always took a couple of days to emerge, following a more detailed official scrutiny. Not until 17 September were details released on the action over Great Britain two days earlier. Then the front page of the *Voelkischer Beobachter* carried the following story:

**NEW LARGE-SCALE ATTACKS BY THE
GERMAN AIR FORCE**
London, Dover, Southampton, Portland, Liverpool
Heavily Bombarded
Gasworks, Oil Storage Areas, Railways Stations,
Factories Producing Military Equipment, Set On Fire
79 British Aircraft Shot Down; Our Own Losses 43

The Military High Command makes it known:
On 15 September and the night to the 16th the reprisal attacks on London continued, under difficult weather conditions. Bombers raided dock and harbour installations, hit Bromley gas works with bombs of the heaviest calibre, set fire to oil tanks and struck railway stations and other targets of military importance in Woolwich and other parts of the city. During the afternoon there was a furious air battle.

The harbour at Dover, oil storage tanks at Portland and an aircraft factory at Southampton were also bombed.

During attacks on convoys off the eastern coasts of Ireland, Scotland and England, two freighters totalling 18,000 tons were sunk. A further ship was set on fire and another was severely damaged . . .

Bombers carried out night attacks on Liverpool and Birmingham and started numerous fires. Mines were laid off British harbours.

During the night British aircraft attempted an attack on the Reich capital, without success. Bombs fell in a few places in western Germany; in one case several houses were destroyed and a school was set on fire. Two civilians were killed and several wounded. Flak and night fighters shot down one aircraft.

Enemy aircraft losses yesterday totalled 79 aircraft; 43 of our own aircraft are missing.

The loss of the ships is confirmed by British records, though, as was often the case when airmen tried to judge tonnage, this was greatly exaggerated: the two ships sunk, the *Nailsea River* and the *Halland*, totalled only 6,800 tons – less than half the German

126

estimate. The ship set on fire was the tug *Grosby*, 212 tons. Two tankers were damaged in air attacks but both reached port.

As in the case of the British victory claim, that issued by the German Air Ministry in Berlin was the total of the claims by aircrews plus the single bomber shot down by flak. Like those issued in London, the German figures had not been inflated for propaganda purposes; again there was no need to, since the figures were good enough as they stood. The claimed destruction of 79 British aircraft was two and a half times greater than the actual British loss of 29 fighters and 1 bomber. The actual number of German planes lost during the attacks on Great Britain, 56, was reduced by 13 before release to the German press.

Like *The Times*, the *Voelkische Beobachter* felt it necessary to stress the veracity of information it published about the war – in contrast to the falsehoods and inventions being published in enemy newspapers:

> A year's experience of war has shown the German people and the rest of the world that one can rely on the truthfulness of the German High Command reports, as one can rely on the predictability of the stars moving across the sky. Our leaders have always stuck to the truth while, in hundreds of instances, the English war reports have been characterized by humbug and lies. In London, even in the direction of military matters, cunning politicians have the last word. If, for example, the number of aircraft the British claim to have shot down was correct, by now the German Air Force would have ceased to exist. The clumsiness and stupidity of Churchill's advisors was shown yet again in yesterday's assertion that the English had shot down 185 German aircraft. The actual loss was 43 machines.

Thus, in the accounts published in the British and German newspapers, both sides claimed a great victory. Each side substantially overclaimed the number of enemy planes destroyed, slightly more so in the British case than the German; and both sides reduced the size of their own losses, more so in the German case than the British. In time of war newspapers were a poor source of information on the conflict; too much was at stake for it to be otherwise.

Chapter 8

IN RETROSPECT

Well, thank God I don't know what it is to lose a battle. But nothing can be more painful than to gain one with the loss of so many friends.
The Duke of Wellington,
after the Battle of Waterloo.

HAVING LOOKED at the events of 15 September 1940 in detail, we shall now consider the importance of the action within the context of the Battle of Britain, and the Battle of Britain within the context of the Second World War.

Each year, 15 September 1940 is commemorated as 'Battle of Britain Day'. One reason for its choice was the 185 German aircraft claimed destroyed; yet, as we now know, that claim was merely the largest in a series of overclaims issued during the Battle. The actual number of German planes destroyed by the defenders on that day, 56, was significantly less than on 15 and 18 August, when 75 and 69 German planes were destroyed respectively.

Yet in historical terms, of the actions fought during the Battle of Britain, only that on 15 September warrants the title 'decisive'. This action convinced Hitler that the Luftwaffe could not gain air superiority over the English Channel in time for an invasion to be launched that year, and led to a postponement of the German plans.

With hindsight, and with details of each side's strength to hand, it might seem odd that as late as the second week in September Hitler thought that Fighter Command could have been defeated within the required time-scale. The reason, discussed in Chapter 1, was that the German intelligence services hugely underestimated the strength of Fighter Command after six weeks of heavy fighting. During the Battle of Britain the

128

Luftwaffe issued victory claims that were just as exaggerated as those of the Royal Air Force. Day after day these claims were subtracted from the estimated numerical strength of Fighter Command, to give a clear impression of the defending fighter force on its last legs. The relatively poor showing by the Royal Air Force against the German daylight attacks on London on 7, 9, 11 and 14 September only confirmed this impression.

All the greater was the impact when, on 15 September, Fighter Command engaged the raiding formations with more than 250 Spitfires and Hurricanes; and it did so not once but twice. The shock effect of this on the Luftwaffe units involved can scarcely be overstated. Horst Schulz flew with Bomber Geschwader 3, the unit hit hardest. He told the author: 'When we got back we all agreed it had been a terrible day, but there was not much discussion. Initially we were grateful for having survived, we were too shaken to think any further than that. Not until the following day did the significance of the one-third losses we had suffered sink in fully. We came to realize that if there were any more missions like that, our chances of survival would be almost nil.'

Roderich Cescotti of Bomber Geschwader 26 commented: 'I regard 15 September as the fiercest battle. None of the other battles in which I was involved made such a profound impression. We were shaken by the number of fighters the Royal Air Force was able to put up on that day, and by the determination of the pilots. It was becoming clear that we were likely to break before the enemy.'

That was not what the Luftwaffe Intelligence Department's assessments had led them to expect. In fact, instead of being on its last legs, Fighter Command was virtually as strong as it had been at the beginning of the Battle.

It was the actions on 15 September that thrust down the throats of the German High Command the unpalatable truth that a victorious outcome to the air fighting over Britain was beyond the grasp of the Luftwaffe. The effect was almost immediate. Two days later Adolf Hitler ordered that Operation Sealion, the planned invasion of England, be postponed 'indefinitely'. Three days after that, on the 20th, reconnaissance Spitfires returned with photographs showing that five destroyers and a torpedo boat had left Cherbourg, and there were fewer barges at the assembly ports. From a peak of more than a thousand barges in the ports between Flushing and Boulogne in mid-September, by the end of the month nearly a third had left. The threat of invasion was past; it would never return.

Yet an important question remains: even if the Luftwaffe had defeated Royal Air Force Fighter Command, could the Germans have mounted a successful invasion of Great Britain?

To carry out a landing on the coast of England, a seaborne invasion force would have had to get past the Royal Navy. During the earlier actions off Norway and elsewhere, almost every capital ship in the German Navy had been sunk or damaged. By September 1940 that force had no battleship or battle-cruiser fit for action. To cover the planned invasion of England it could muster only 1 heavy cruiser, 3 light cruisers, 9 destroyers and about 30 U-boats. In contrast, to counter such an attempt, the Royal Navy had assembled 5 battleships, 11 cruisers, 43 destroyers and 35 submarines in home ports, all ready to go to sea at short notice.

Some commentators have expressed the view that if the Luftwaffe could have gained a sufficiently high degree of air superiority over the English Channel and southern England, that might have redressed the huge disparity between the two sides' navies. Such a view does not withstand analysis.

At that time the Luftwaffe had no effective torpedo-bomber force. Only a few low-performance Heinkel 115 floatplanes were equipped for the role, and the type of torpedo they carried was known to be unreliable. High-level attacks on manoeuvring warships by horizontal bombers were notoriously ineffective, and would not have caused the Royal Navy any great embarrassment. During the Dunkirk evacuation dive-bombers had proved formidably effective against cruisers and destroyers; but the Luftwaffe possessed no bombs that would penetrate the deck armour of battleships. Moreover, for a successful dive-bombing attack the sky had to be clear up to at least 8,000 feet; that condition could not be guaranteed over the English Channel, especially after the second week in September. Unless there were exceptional moonlight conditions, the Luftwaffe had no effective night attack capability against warships manoeuvring in open water.

Given these limitations, the Royal Navy's tactics in the event of an invasion can be predicted with confidence. Warships making their way to the German landing areas would probably have timed their passage to arrive at first light, having made their approach during the hours of darkness when they were almost invulnerable to air attack. Once off the invasion area, the immensely powerful Royal Navy forces could have brushed aside the German escorts and annihilated the assemblies of unarmed merchant ships and invasion barges.

No less an authority than Dietrich Peltz, a dive-bombing expert and later Inspector General of Bombers in the Luftwaffe, has told the author that in his view the Luftwaffe could not have prevented the Royal Navy from wrecking the German invasion fleet. Vice-Admiral Kurt Assmann, a German naval expert, put it another way: 'Had the Luftwaffe defeated the Royal Air Force as decisively as it had defeated the French Air Force a few months earlier, I am sure Hitler would have given the order for the invasion to be launched – and the invasion would in all probability have been smashed.'

The order was never given. A seaborne invasion operation against Britain, precarious enough even with Fighter Command neutralized, would have been suicidal if it was not.

Just over 140 years earlier, in a Britain similarly under threat of invasion from France, the First Lord of the Admiralty was moved to comment, 'I do not say the Frenchmen will not come; I only say they will not come by sea.' If the German troops could not have come by sea, could they have come by air? Again, the prospects of success were poor.

The German use of airborne troops to spearhead the invasion of Holland, just over four months earlier, had introduced a new dimension into warfare. But the boldness and success of that enterprise masked the manifest weaknesses of this type of operation. First, a large fleet of Junkers 52 transport planes was necessary to carry the troops into action. Following heavy losses inflicted on the transport planes during the campaign in Holland, the Luftwaffe possessed less than three hundred of these aircraft. To lift into action a parachute division of 8,000 men required about 900 sorties by Ju 52s – that is to say at least three sorties from each available plane, with no allowance for losses. That, just to land one infantry division with no heavy weapons.

Moreover, to maintain that airborne division in action would have entailed a re-supply operation delivering about a hundred tons of food, ammunition and other supplies *per day*. The

131

Junkers 52 carried a maximum load of about three tons, but if the load was to be air-dropped the maximum was reduced to about two tons. Thus to re-supply the division it would have required about sixty Ju 52 sorties per day if the loads were air-dropped, or forty per day if an airfield was captured and the planes could land to offload. The re-supply operation would have had to continue indefinitely. Again no allowance has been made for losses, though the slow-moving transports would have been vulnerable to attacks from the tattered remnant of an otherwise-defeated Fighter Command.

All in all, it is clear that an airborne invasion of England unsupported by seaborne forces would have failed even more disastrously than the British airborne operation at Arnhem four years later. The British Army might have been weak immediately after the Dunkirk evacuation, but it was never so weak that it could not have overwhelmed a German force landed and supplied from the air.

To sum up: in 1940 the Germans lacked the naval strength to secure the passage for seaborne landings in England, and they lacked the transport aircraft to lift into battle and keep supplied an airborne force that would survive for more than the briefest of periods.

If a successful invasion of Great Britain was highly unlikely whatever the outcome of the Battle of Britain, did Fighter Command make a significant contribution to the nation's survival? Without doubt, it did.

At the time many people on both sides thought the German bombers could have inflicted damage and casualties on such a scale that the British Government would have been forced to sue for peace. In that event the risky invasion operation would not be necessary. Had Fighter Command been knocked out as an effective fighting force, and had the Luftwaffe been able to employ its large fleet of bombers to deliver a series of accurate and devastating daylight attacks on Britain's cities, it is just possible that this could have led to a collapse of civilian morale. Then, a British Government might have been forced to accede to the German peace terms. As everyone knows, none of those things happened.

Yet transcending even that was the boost to national morale provided by the Royal Air Force's victory in the Battle of Britain.

The previous spring had seen a series of unparalleled military disasters for Great Britain and her allies. Denmark, Norway, Holland, Belgium and France had all fallen to the enemy in rapid succession. It seemed that nothing had gone right. Britain now stood alone, but could she do so for long against so formidable an adversary? The Battle of Britain demonstrated, for the first time, that the German war machine was not invincible. The way ahead was long and it was hard, but it need not end in defeat. That knowledge was the most important thing to result from the Battle of Britain.

Chapter 9

CONFLICTING EVIDENCE

So little trouble do men take in the search after truth; so readily do they accept whatever comes first to hand.

Thucydides

THE AUTHOR believes that the account in this book is the most accurate ever published on the events of 15 September 1940. Other books and publications describing this day contain information that is at variance with the author's findings, however. This chapter examines some of the areas where evidence is conflicting, to enable the reader to decide which account to accept.

How many German aircraft were shot down on 15 September 1940?
The Luftwaffe admitted losing 43 aircraft on that day, and that figure was published in the German press. Although the official German figure is usually ignored by historians, this was much closer to the truth than the figure that appeared in the British press.

In the evening of 15 September the Air Ministry in London released its figures for the number of German aircraft destroyed that day: 178 shot down by fighters, 7 destroyed by anti-aircraft fire. In addition, 40 German planes were claimed 'probably destroyed' and 25 damaged.

When the Luftwaffe loss records were captured in 1945, the number of planes that service lost on 15 September 1940 was shown to be less than one-third the number claimed by the British defences. So, how many aircraft did the defences shoot down that day? The figure most published is 60, and that number appears in the official history, *The Defence of the United Kingdom*. Analysis of German documents reveals that this figure

134

is too high, however. It includes two Junkers 88s (both belonging to Bomber Geschwader 51) lost during the early morning darkness on the 16th. And it includes a couple of seaplanes, a Dornier 18 and a Heinkel 59, lost in separate accidents while alighting on the sea well clear of the enemy. Deleting these four aircraft from the total brings the number of German planes destroyed in action during the day to 56, and the author offers this as the most accurate figure. In addition, 23 German aircraft returned with damage which, in two cases, was beyond repair.

How many Royal Air Force aircraft were shot down on 15 September 1940?
The initial press releases issued by the Air Ministry in London stated that 30 British fighters had been lost in the action, one more than actually lost. For some reason, later press releases amended the figure for British fighters lost to 25. The reported loss of 12 Royal Air Force pilots killed was accurate. Luftwaffe units claimed 79 British planes destroyed that day, and it is interesting to note that this figure was inflated by almost the same factor as the British claim for German aircraft destroyed.

Did the Luftwaffe employ the major part of its forces during the attacks on 15 September 1940?
Several accounts of the Battle of Britain state that on 15 September the Luftwaffe sent all, or most, of its available bombers and fighters against London. From German records, however, it is clear that only 162 bombers were sent against London, and that included 21 single-engined Messerschmitt 109 fighter-bombers. The force sent against Portland numbered 26 and that against Southampton was 13. Thus a total of 201 bombers of all types took part in the four main daylight attacks. On that day the Luftwaffe possessed about 800 serviceable twin-engined bombers, plus about 44 Me 109s and Me 110s belonging to fighter-bomber units. Thus only about a quarter of the serviceable bombers of Air Fleets 2 and 3 were sent against England during the daylight hours of 15 September.

The German single-engined fighter force *was* fully committed on 15 September. On that day Air Fleets 2 and 3 possessed about 620 serviceable Messerschmitt 109s, and these flew 769 sorties against England. The great majority of those sorties were flown by Air Fleet 2, however, from its force of 530 single-engined fighters. Thus the latter's single-engined fighter units flew an average of 1.45 sorties per aircraft that day, most of them to the limit of the Me 109s' endurance. During the two large-scale attacks on London, Air Fleet 2's fighter force was at full stretch.

Messerschmitt 110 twin-engined fighters played relatively little part in the actions of 15 September. Air Fleet 2 possessed about 90 of these aircraft serviceable, but it is estimated that they flew only about 40 sorties over England.

Did RAF fighters succeed in breaking up or turning back any German formations on 15 September 1940?
Several accounts of the action on 15 September mention German formations having been 'broken up' and raids 'turned back' by RAF fighters. British wartime narratives often mention the break-up of German formations, the implication being that bomber crews lacking the stomach to continue with their attack could save themselves by leaving formation and running for home alone. Nothing could be further from the truth. To break out of a formation under attack from fighters was the most dangerous course, as German crews were fully aware. The only bombers to leave formations under attack had suffered mechanical failure or battle damage and were physically unable to remain in formation. The reader has seen several examples where bombers were forced out of formation and tried to make their way home alone; relatively few succeeded.

There is a similar misconception about German bomber formations having been turned back by fighter attacks. Unless his force had lost more than half its aircraft – and none did so on 15 September – no unit commander would turn back in such circumstances. To do so would mean the risk of having to repeat the attack or, at worst, facing a court martial for cowardice in the face of the enemy. RAF fighters did not force bomber formations to turn back, but cloud cover over targets, preventing accurate bombing, often did; we have seen instances of this during the afternoon action. No German bomber formation was broken up or turned back by RAF fighters on 15 September.

What role did Ultra play during the action on 15 September 1940?
Since the post-war revelation of the British Ultra cipher-breaking operation, some accounts have implied that information from this source governed the tactical handling of Fighter Command

during the Battle of Britain. It has even been suggested that Winston Churchill's visit to No. 11 Group Headquarters on the morning of 15 September was evidence that he knew from Ultra that the Luftwaffe planned to launch heavy attacks on London that day.

The most detailed and reliable account of the part played by Ultra in the Battle of Britain is in Volume 1 of the official history, *British Intelligence in the Second World War*, by F. H. Hinsley. That author makes it clear that although Ultra provided useful intelligence on the Luftwaffe during the summer of 1940, it came in the form of fragmentary and often disconnected items that were rarely of immediate use to C.-in-C. Fighter Command. Only a small proportion of the Luftwaffe signals traffic was sent by wireless telegraphy (W/T), and relatively little of that was being decrypted and read by British Intelligence. Professor Hinsley has written that this source was no help in forecasting the shifts that occurred during the Battle in the Luftwaffe's methods and objectives:

> Communications between Berlin and the GAF [German Air Force] formations in France went by land-lines, so that strategic decisions were rarely spelled out in W/T signals. From time to time it could be deduced from the decrypts that a change in the GAF's intentions was to be expected, but the deductions were of no operational value to the C.-in-C. Fighter Command. For one thing, there was no knowing how widely they applied – for not all the forward GAF formations used W/T. For another, they were too vague.

As an example of the latter, Professor Hinsley stated that between 9 and 13 August several decrypted signals referred to 'Adlertag'. But neither the code breakers at Bletchley Park nor Air Intelligence could discover the meaning of 'Adlertag', though clearly it referred to a major operation. Only after the operation was launched was it realized that the code-word referred to the large-scale air attack on targets in Great Britain.

There were other limitations to the value of information from Ultra, which in practice prevented Air Chief Marshal Dowding placing any great reliance on this source when disposing his forces to meet attacks. Hinsley continued:

> In the day-to-day fighting, by giving notice of the time, the targets and the forces committed to individual raids, [Ultra]

provided an increasing amount of intelligence as the GAF moved into its all-out effort. But this intelligence was sometimes obtained too late to be of operational value. Moreover, the GAF made last-minute alterations of plan which were not disclosed in the decrypts, or were not disclosed in good time. As an example of this difficulty, which sometimes undermined confidence in the source, [Ultra] decrypts revealed on 14 September that a big raid on London was to take place that day, and gave an indication of the forces that would take part in it; but they had previously announced that the raid was scheduled for 1800 [hours] on 13 September, and in the event the raid was made on the morning of 15 September without any further [Ultra] warning.

It appears certain that the first reliable indication Fighter Command had of the attacks on 15 September was when the leading elements of the German forces appeared on radar.

Winston Churchill's visit to No. 11 Group Headquarters on 15 September cannot be taken as evidence that he had warning from Ultra of the Luftwaffe attack on London that day. During the Battle Mr Churchill frequently visited Park's headquarters. By the second week in September the Luftwaffe was launching heavy attacks against England whenever the weather permitted. A forecast of reasonable weather over the south-east of the country on the 15th meant that a German attack was likely, and that would have been reason enough for the Prime Minister to visit Uxbridge.

Was the action of 15 September won by a narrow margin?
It is an established part of the folklore of the Battle of Britain that Fighter Command won by only a narrow margin. Certainly its squadrons took heavy knocks during the battle, but so had the enemy. On 15 September the Command mounted an extremely effective defence of the capital using almost all its Category A squadrons. But in fact *less than half* its serviceable Spitfires and Hurricanes were committed. Although the Category A day-fighter squadrons based in the south-east of England were at full stretch on that day, Fighter Command still retained a significant reserve of aircraft and experienced pilots that had not been committed. Had the day's battle gone badly, we should have seen an influx of pilots and fighters from the northern and western areas to replenish the squadrons in the south-east. It would have taken more than a single reverse, no matter how severe, to put Fighter Command out of the Battle.

Appendix A

EQUIVALENT RANKS

Royal Air Force	Luftwaffe
Marshal of the Royal Air Force	Generalfeldmarschall
Air Chief Marshal	Generaloberst
Air Marshal	General
Air Vice-Marshal	Generalleutnant
Air Commodore	Generalmajor
Group Captain	Oberst
Wing Commander	Oberstleutnant
Squadron Leader	Major
Flight Lieutenant	Hauptmann
Flying Officer	Oberleutnant
Pilot Officer	Leutnant
Warrant Officer	Stabsfeldwebel
Flight Sergeant	Oberfeldwebel
Sergeant	Feldwebel
Corporal	Unteroffizier
Leading Aircraftman	Obergefreiter
Aircraftman First Class	Gefreiter
Aircraftman Second Class	Flieger

Appendix B

AIRCRAFT IN ACTION ON
15 SEPTEMBER 1940

ROYAL AIR FORCE

Bristol Blenheim The most numerous night-fighter type in service with the Royal Air Force. Crew: pilot and gunner. Some fitted with Airborne Interception radar, in which case a radar operator was also carried. Two 840 h.p. Bristol Mercury engines. Maximum speed: 285 m.p.h. Armament: five .303-in. machine guns firing forwards, one .303-in. machine gun in fuselage turret.

Hawker Hurricane The most numerous fighter type in the Royal Air Force. Single seater. One 1,030 h.p. Rolls-Royce Merlin engine. Maximum speed: 328 m.p.h. Armament: eight .303-in. machine guns.

Supermarine Spitfire The highest-performance fighter type in the Royal Air Force. Single seater. (Mark I) one 1,030 h.p. Rolls-Royce Merlin, maximum speed 345 m.p.h.; (Mark II) one 1,140 h.p. RR Merlin, maximum speed 354 m.p.h. Armament: eight .303-in. machine guns.

Bristol Beaufighter Just entering service with night-fighter units. Crew: pilot and radar operator. Two 1,400 h.p. Bristol Hercules engines. Maximum speed 321 m.p.h. Armament: four 20 mm cannon, six .303-in. machine guns.

LUFTWAFFE

Dornier 17 Two 1,000 h.p. Bramo engines. Crew: pilot, navigator/ bomb aimer/front gunner, wireless operator/rear gunner and flight engineer/underneath gunner. Sometimes a fifth man was carried to operate the guns firing from each side of the cabin. Although this type was still in large-scale service in the Luftwaffe, production had ceased and it was being replaced by the Junkers 88. Cruising speed in formation: 180 m.p.h. Armament: up to five 7.9 mm machine guns. Typical bomb loads: four 550-pound *or* twenty 110-pound high-explosive bombs.

Heinkel 111 The heaviest of the German twin-engined bomber types operating during the Battle of Britain. Crew: pilot, navigator/bomb aimer/front gunner, radio operator/rear gunner and flight engineer/ underneath gunner. Sometimes a fifth man was carried to operate the guns firing from each side of the fuselage. Two 1,100 h.p. Daimler Benz engines. Cruising speed, in formation: 180 m.p.h. Armament: up to six 7.9 mm machine guns in separate mountings. Typical bomb loads: six 550-pound bombs *or* two 550-pounders, one 550-pound incendiary cluster and twelve 110-pound high-explosive bombs.

Junkers 88 The most modern German bomber type operational during the Battle of Britain, employed on 15 September mainly for night attacks but also for nuisance raids by day. Crew: pilot, navigator/bomb aimer, front gunner, wireless operator/rear gunner and flight engineer/underneath gunner. Two 1,200 h.p. Daimler Benz engines. Cruising speed in formation, 180 m.p.h. Armament up to four 7.9 mm machine guns in separate mountings. Typical bomb loads: four 550-pound bombs *or* one 1,100-pounder and two 550-pound bombs. Also served in the photographic reconnaissance role during the Battle.

Messerschmitt 109 One 1,150 h.p. Daimler Benz engine. Single seater. The sole single-engined fighter type operated by the Luftwaffe during the Battle of Britain. Maximum speed: 354 m.p.h. Armament: two 20 mm cannon, two 7.9 mm machine guns. This type also served in the fighter-bomber role that day, carrying four 110-pound bombs *or* one 550-pound incendiary bomb.

Messerschmitt 110 Two 1,150 h.p. Daimler Benz engines. Crew: pilot and wireless operator/rear gunner. The most numerous twin-engined fighter type in the Luftwaffe. Maximum speed: 349 m.p.h. Armament: two 20 mm cannon and four 7.9 mm machine guns firing forwards, one 7.9 mm machine gun firing aft. Also served in the fighter-bomber role that day, carrying two 1,100-pound bombs, and in the photographic reconnaissance role.

Appendix C

LUFTWAFFE ORDER OF BATTLE

Units deployed to attack Great Britain, 7 September 1940. First figure, aircraft serviceable; second figure, aircraft unserviceable. Note: Luftwaffe unit strength returns were compiled at ten-day intervals. This Appendix gives the return on 7 September, the last one before the action on the 15th.

LUFTFLOTTE 2, HQ BRUSSELS
Long-Range Bombers

Bomber Geschwader 1

Staff Flight	Heinkel 111	5	2	Rosierès-en-Santerre
I Gruppe	Heinkel 111	22	14	Montdidier, Clairmont
II Gruppe	Heinkel 111	23	13	Montdidier, Nijmegen
III Gruppe	Junkers 88	–	9	Rosierès-en-Santerre

Bomber Geschwader 2

Staff Flight	Dornier 17	6	0	Saint-Leger
I Gruppe	Dornier 17	12	7	Cambrai
II Gruppe	Dornier 17	20	11	Saint-Leger
III Gruppe	Dornier 17	20	10	Cambrai

Bomber Geschwader 3

Staff Flight	Dornier 17	5	1	Le Culot
I Gruppe	Dornier 17	25	4	Le Culot
II Gruppe	Dornier 17	23	4	Antwerp/Deurne
III Gruppe	Dornier 17	19	9	Saint-Trond

Bomber Geschwader 4

Staff Flight	Heinkel 111	5	5	Soesterberg
I Gruppe	Heinkel 111	16	21	Soesterberg
II Gruppe	Heinkel 111	30	7	Eindhoven
III Gruppe	Junkers 88	14	16	Amsterdam/Schipol

Bomber Geschwader 26

Staff Flight	Heinkel 111	3	3	Gilze-Rijen
I Gruppe	Heinkel 111	7	18	Moerbeke, Coutrai (operated from Wevelghem on 15 September)
II Gruppe	Heinkel 111	7	19	Gilze-Rijen

Bomber Geschwader 30

Staff Flight	Junkers 88	1	–	Brussels
I Gruppe	Junkers 88	1	9	Brussels
II Gruppe	Junkers 88	24	6	Gilze-Rijen

Bomber Geschwader 40

Staff Flight	FW 200	1	1	Bordeaux

Bomber Geschwader 53

Staff Flight	Heinkel 111	3	2	Lille
I Gruppe	Heinkel 111	19	4	Lille
II Gruppe	Heinkel 111	7	22	Lille
III Gruppe	Heinkel 111	4	15	Lille

Bomber Geschwader 76

Staff Flight	Dornier 17	3	3	Cormeilles-en-Vexin
I Gruppe	Dornier 17	19	7	Beauvais/Tille
II Gruppe	Junkers 88	21	6	Creil
III Gruppe	Dornier 17	17	7	Cormeilles-en-Vexin

Bomber Geschwader 77

Staff Flight	Junkers 88	1	–	Laon
I Gruppe	Junkers 88	31	5	Laon
II Gruppe	Junkers 88	25	7	Asch
III Gruppe	Junkers 88	19	11	Laon

Bomber Gruppe 126

	Heinkel 111	26	7	Marx

Dive-Bombers and Fighter-Bombers

Dive-Bomber Geschwader 1

Staff Flight	Ju 87, Do 17	5	2	Saint-Pol
II Gruppe	Junkers 87	29	14	Pas-de-Calais

Dive-Bomber Geschwader 2

Staff Flight	Ju 87, Do 17	9	2	Tramecourt
II Gruppe	Junkers 87	22	5	Saint-Omer, Saint-Trond

Lehr Geschwader 1

IV Gruppe	Junkers 87	28	14	Tramecourt

Lehr Geschwader 2

II Gruppe	Me 109	27	5	Saint-Omer (fighter-bomber unit)

Single-Engined Fighters

Fighter Geschwader 1

Staff Flight	Me 109	3	1	Pas de Calais area

Fighter Geschwader 3

Staff Flight	Me 109	3	–	Samer
I Gruppe	Me 109	14	9	Samer
II Gruppe	Me 109	21	3	Samer
III Gruppe	Me 109	23	2	Desvres

Fighter Geschwader 26

Staff Flight	Me 109	3	1	Audembert
I Gruppe	Me 109	20	7	Audembert
II Gruppe ·	Me 109	28	4	Marquise
III Gruppe	Me 109	26	3	Caffiers

Fighter Geschwader 27

Staff Flight	Me 109	4	1	Etaples
I Gruppe	Me 109	27	6	Etaples
II Gruppe	Me 109	33	4	Montreuil
III Gruppe	Me 109	27	4	Sempy

Fighter Geschwader 51

Staff Flight	Me 109	4	1	Saint-Omer
I Gruppe	Me 109	33	3	Saint-Omer, Saint-Inglevert
II Gruppe	Me 109	13	9	Saint-Omer, Saint-Inglevert
III Gruppe	Me 109	31	13	Saint-Omer

Fighter Geschwader 52

Staff Flight	Me 109	1	1	Laon/Couvron
I Gruppe	Me 109	17	4	Laon/Couvron
II Gruppe	Me·109	23	5	Pas-de-Calais area
III Gruppe	Me 109	16	15	Pas-de-Calais area

Fighter Geschwader 53

Staff Flight	Me 1)9	2	–	Pas-de-Calais area
II Gruppe	Me 109	24	9	Wissant
III Gruppe	Me 109	22	8	Pas-de-Calais area

Fighter Geschwader 54

Staff Flight	Me 109	2	2	Holland
I Gruppe	Me 109	23	5	Holland
II Gruppe	Me 109	27	8	Holland
III Gruppe	Me 109	23	5	Holland

Fighter Geschwader 77

I Gruppe	Me 109	40	2	Pas-de-Calais area

Twin-Engined Fighters

Destroyer Geschwader 2

Staff Flight	Me 110	–	1	Pas-de-Calais area
I Gruppe	Me 110	10	10	Amiens, Caen
II Gruppe	Me 110	10	18	Guyancourt/Caudran

Destroyer Geschwader 26

Staff Flight	Me 110	3	–	Lille
I Gruppe	Me 110	14	19	Abbeville, Saint-Omer
II Gruppe	Me 110	17	8	Crécy
III Gruppe	Me 110	17	8	Barley, Arques

Lehr Geschwader 1

V Gruppe	Me 110	19	4	Ligescourt, Alençon

Erprobungs Gruppe 210

	Me 109, Me 110	17	9	Denain (fighter- bomber unit)

Long-Range Reconnaissance

Long-Range Reconnaissance Gruppe 22

1 Staffel	Do 17, Me 110	9	4	Lille

Long Range Reconnaissance Gruppe 122

1 Staffel	Junkers 88	3	5	Holland
2 Staffel	Ju 88, He 111	9	1	Brussels/Melsbroek
3 Staffel	Ju 88, He 111	10	1	Eindhoven
4 Staffel	Ju 88, He 111, Me 110	9	4	Brussels
5 Staffel	Ju 88, He 111	11	–	Haute-Fontain

Maritime Reconnaissance and Minelaying Aircraft

Coastal Flying Gruppe 106

1 Staffel	Heinkel 115	4	6	Brittany area
2 Staffel	Dornier 18	6	3	Brittany area
3 Staffel	Heinkel 115	6	3	Borkum

AIR FLEET 3, HQ PARIS
Long-Range Bombers

Lehr Geschwader 1

Staff Flight	Junkers 88	3	–	Orléans/Bricy
I Gruppe	Junkers 88	13	14	Orléans/Bricy
II Gruppe	Junkers 88	19	12	Orléans/Bricy
III Gruppe	Junkers 88	19	11	Chateaudun

Bomber Geschwader 27

Staff Flight	Heinkel 111	4	3	Tours
I Gruppe	Heinkel 111	13	22	Tours
II Gruppe	Heinkel 111	15	17	Dinard, Bourges
III Gruppe	Heinkel 111	13	7	Rennes

Bomber Geschwader 40

I Gruppe	FW 200	4	3	Bordeaux

Bomber Geschwader 51

Staff Flight	Junkers 88	–	1	Orly
I Gruppe	Junkers 88	13	20	Melun
II Gruppe	Junkers 88	17	17	Orly
III Gruppe	Junkers 88	27	7	Etampes

Bomber Geschwader 54

Staff Flight	Junkers 88	–	1	Evreux
I Gruppe	Junkers 88	18	12	Evreux
II Gruppe	Junkers 88	14	12	St-André

Bomber Geschwader 55

Staff Flight	Heinkel 111	6	–	Villacoublay
I Gruppe	Heinkel 111	20	7	Dreux

II Gruppe	Heinkel 111	22	8	Chartres
III Gruppe	Heinkel 111	20	5	Villacoublay
Bomber Gruppe 100				
	Heinkel 111	7	21	Vannes
Bomber Gruppe 606				
	Dornier 17	29	4	Brest, Cherbourg
Bomber Gruppe 806				
	Junkers 88	18	9	Nantes, Caen

Dive-Bombers

Dive-Bomber Geschwader 3				
Staff Flt	Do 17, He 111	6	1	Brittany area
I Gruppe	Junkers 87	34	3	Brittany area

Single-Engined Fighters

Fighter Geschwader 2				
Staff Flight	Me 109	2	3	Beaumont-le-Roger
I Gruppe	Me 109	24	5	Beaumont-le-Roger
II Gruppe	Me 109	18	4	Beaumont-le-Roger
III Gruppe	Me 109	19	11	Le Havre
Fighter Geschwader 53				
I Gruppe	Me 109	27	7	Brittany area

Twin-Engined Fighters

Destroyer Geschwader 76				
Staff Flight	Me 110	2	2	
II Gruppe	Me 110	12	15	Le Mans, Abbeville
III Gruppe	Me 110	8	11	Laval

Long-Range Reconnaissance

Lehr Geschwader 2				
7 Staffel	Me 110	9	5	
Reconnaissance Gruppe 14				
4 Staffel	Me 110, Do 17	9	3	Normandy area
Reconnaissance Gruppe 31				
3 Staffel	Me 110, Do 17	5	4	St-Brieuc
Reconnaissance Gruppe 121				
3 Staffel	Ju 88, He 111	6	4	North-west France
4 Staffel	Ju 88, Do 17	5	8	Normandy
Reconnaissance Gruppe 123				
1 Staffel	Ju 88, Do 17	7	3	Paris area
2 Staffel	Ju 88, Do 17	8	2	Paris area
3 Staffel	Ju 88, Do 17	9	3	Buc

AIR FLEET 5, HQ KRISTIANSUND, NORWAY
Single-Engined Fighters

Fighter Geschwader 77				
II Gruppe	Me 109	35	9	Southern Norway

Long-Range Reconnaissance

Reconnaissance Gruppe 22

2 Staffel	Dornier 17	5	4	Stavanger
3 Staffel	Dornier 17	5	4	Stavanger

Reconnaissance Gruppe 120

1 Staffel	He 111, Ju 88	2	11	Stavanger

Reconnaissance Gruppe 121

1 Staffel	He 111, Ju 88	2	5	Stavanger, Aalborg

Maritime Reconnaissance and Minelaying Aircraft

Coastal Flying Gruppe 506

1 Staffel	Heinkel 115	6	2	Stavanger
2 Staffel	Heinkel 115	5	3	Trondheim, Tromsö
3 Staffel	Heinkel 115	6	2	List

Appendix D

ROYAL AIR FORCE FIGHTER COMMAND ORDER OF BATTLE

Fighter Command Units, 6 p.m. 14 September 1940. First figure, aircraft serviceable; second figure, aircraft unserviceable

No. 10 Group, HQ Box, Wiltshire

Middle Wallop Sector

238 Squadron	Hurricanes	17	1	Middle Wallop
609 Squadron	Spitfires	15	3	Middle Wallop
604 Squadron	Blenheims	5	14	Middle Wallop
	Beaufighters	–	1	Middle Wallop
Half 23 Squadron	Blenheims	6	–	Middle Wallop
152 Squadron	Spitfires	17	2	Warmwell
56 Squadron	Hurricanes	17	–	Boscombe Down

Filton Sector

79 Squadron	Hurricanes	13	5	Pembrey

Exeter Sector

87 Squadron	Hurricanes	17	4	Exeter
601 Squadron	Hurricanes	14	6	Exeter

St Eval Sector

234 Squadron	Spitfires	16	1	St Eval
247 Squadron	Gladiators	9	–	Roborough

No. 11 Group, HQ Uxbridge, Middlesex

Kenley Sector

253 Squadron	Hurricanes	14	3	Kenley
501 Squadron	Hurricanes	18	1	Kenley
605 Squadron	Hurricanes	16	3	Croydon

Biggin Hill Sector

72 Squadron	Spitfires	10	7	Biggin Hill
92 Squadron	Spitfires	16	1	Biggin Hill
Half 141 Squadron	Defiants	10	–	Biggin Hill
66 Squadron	Spitfires	14	2	Gravesend

Northolt Sector

1 RCAF Squadron	Hurricanes	15	3	Northolt
229 Squadron	Hurricanes	19	–	Northolt
303 Polish Squadron	Hurricanes	15	4	Northolt

Half 264 Squadron	Defiants	8	–	Northolt
504 Squadron	Hurricanes	15	–	Hendon
Hornchurch Sector				
603 Squadron	Spitfires	14	5	Hornchurch
600 Squadron	Blenheims	13	5	Hornchurch
	Beaufighters	6	6	Hornchurch
41 Squadron	Spitfires	12	6	Rochford
222 Squadron	Spitfires	11	3	Rochford
North Weald Sector				
257 Squadron	Hurricanes	14	4	Martlesham Heath
Half 25 Squadron	Blenheims	5	5	Martlesham Heath
249 Squadron	Hurricanes	17	1	North Weald
Half 23 Squadron	Blenheims	7	5	North Weald
	Beaufighters	5	–	North Weald
46 Squadron	Hurricanes	14	3	Stapleford Tawney
Debden Sector				
17 Squadron	Hurricanes	15	3	Debden
73 Squadron	Hurricanes	14	–	Castle Camps
Tangmere Sector				
213 Squadron	Hurricanes	13	6	Tangmere
607 Squadron	Hurricanes	19	1	Tangmere
602 Squadron	Spitfires	15	4	Westhampnett
Half 23 Squadron	Blenheims	10	5	Ford
	Beaufighters	1	–	Ford

No. 12 Group, HQ Watnall, Nottinghamshire

Duxford Sector				
242 Squadron	Hurricanes	17	–	Duxford
310 Czech Squadron	Hurricanes	18	2	Duxford ·
312 Czech Squadron	Hurricanes	4	5	Duxford (non-operational)
19 Squadron	Spitfires	14	–	Fowlmere
Coltishall Sector				
74 Squadron	Spitfires	14	8	Coltishall
Wittering Sector				
1 Squadron	Hurricanes	16	2	Wittering
266 Squadron	Spitfires	14	5	Wittering
Digby Sector				
611 Squadron	Spitfires	17	1	Digby (to Fowlmere, morning 15th)
151 Squadron	Hurricanes	17	1	Digby
29 Squadron	Blenheims	16	5	Digby
	Beaufighters	1	–	Digby

Kirton in Lindsey Sector

616 Squadron	Spitfires	14	4	Kirton in Lindsey
Half 264 Squadron	Defiants	6	4	Kirton in Lindsey
307 Polish Squadron	Defiants	8	8	Kirton in Lindsey (forming)

Church Fenton Sector

85 Squadron	Hurricanes	17	1	Church Fenton
306 Polish Squadron	Hurricanes	4	5	Church Fenton (one flight operational)
302 Polish Squadron	Hurricanes	16	2	Leconfield (moved to Duxford early on 15th)
64 Squadron	Spitfires	7	3	Leconfield
		6	3	Ringway

No. 13 Group, HQ Newcastle, Northumberland

Catterick Sector

54 Squadron	Spitfires	15	2	Catterick
Half 219 Squadron	Blenheims	8	4	Catterick
	Beaufighters	–	1	Catterick

Usworth Sector

43 Squadron	Hurricanes	13	1	Usworth
32 Squadron	Hurricanes	14	1	Acklington
610 Squadron	Spitfires	4	5	Acklington
Half 219 Squadron	Blenheims	6	1	Acklington

Turnhouse Sector

3 Squadron	Hurricanes	15	3	Turnhouse
65 Squadron	Spitfires	15	5	Turnhouse
Half 141 Squadron	Defiants	7	4	Turnhouse
615 Squadron	Hurricanes	16	6	Prestwick
111 Squadron	Hurricanes	24	2	Drem
263 Squadron	Hurricanes	8	4	Drem
	Whirlwinds	4	3	non-operational

Dyce Sector

145 Squadron	Hurricanes	13	8	Dyce

Wick Sector

232 Squadron	Hurricanes	7	1	Sumburgh

Aldergrove Sector

245 Squadron	Hurricanes	18	4	Aldergrove

Fighter Aircraft at Operational Training Units, 14 September

Spitfires	26	24
Hurricanes	47	40
Defiants	3	5
Blenheims	16	9

Fighter Aircraft held at Maintenance Units, 14 September

Ready for Immediate Use		Ready in Four Days
Spitfires	47	10
Hurricanes	80	17
Defiants	81	1
Beaufighters	1	7

Fighter Production in Britain, during week prior to 14 September

Spitfires	38
Hurricanes	56
Defiants	10
Beaufighters	4

Appendix E

MAIN ATTACKS ON GREAT BRITAIN, 15 SEPTEMBER 1940

Time of Attack	Target Attacked	Unit(s)	Attacking Force	Remarks
Midnight	London	BGr 606	13 Do 17	In progress at midnight.
0.15 a.m.	London	BG 51	2 Ju 88	Night attack.
0.50 a.m.	London	BGr 126	11 He 111	As above.
2.00 a.m.	London	BG 4	5 He 111	Night attack planned for 46 bombers. Operation curtailed owing to bad weather over bases in Holland.
11.50 a.m.	London	II/LG 2	21 Me 109	Attack by fighter-bombers.
12.10 p.m.	London	I&III/BG 76	25 Do 17	Attacked rail viaducts at Battersea.
2.45 p.m.	London	I&II/BG 53	20 He 111	Intended target, R. Victoria Dock, could not be attacked owing to cloud. Bombed West Ham area instead.
2.48 p.m.	London	II/BG 3	11 Do 17	As above.
2.50 p.m.	London	I&II/BG 26	27 He 111	Intended target West India Dock. Bombed Bromley-by-Bow gas works instead.

Abbreviations: BG – Bomber Geschwader   BGr – Bomber Gruppe
LG – Lehr Geschwader   EGr – Erprobungs Gruppe
I&III/BG 55 – Ist and IIIrd Gruppen of Bomber Geschwader 55

Time of Attack	Target Attacked	Unit(s)	Attacking Force	Remarks
2.55 p.m.	London	II&III/BG 2	42 Do 17	Intended target Surrey Commercial Dock. Bombed targets of opportunity in SE London and Kent instead.
3.30 p.m.	Portland	I&III/BG 55	26 He 111	RN dockyard.
5.30 p.m.	South-ampton	EGr 210	10 Me 110 3 Me 109	Attack by fighter-bombers. Target Supermarine Aircraft factory. Bombs missed target and fell on built-up area nearby.
8.00 p.m.	London	BGr 806	7 Ju 88	Night attack.
8.50 p.m.	London	III/LG 1	10 Ju 88	As above.
9.05 p.m.	London	II/BG 55	15 He 111	As above.
9.46 p.m.	London	I/LG 1	10 Ju 88	As above.
10.25 p.m.	London	St&I/BG 55	5 He 111	As above.
10.45 p.m.	London	III/BG 27	11 He 111	As above.
10.48 p.m.	Liverpool	II/BG 27	9 He 111	As above.
11.12 p.m.	London	I/BG 54	10 Ju 88	As above.
11.32 p.m.	London	I/BG 27	18 He 111	As above.
11.50 p.m.	London	II/BG 51	8 Ju 88	As above.

GERMAN COMBAT LOSSES, 15 SEPTEMBER 1940

In this section a 'combat loss' is any aircraft destroyed or damaged while engaged in a combat sortie, whatever the cause. Where these are known, the list includes the works number of the aircraft and the name of the pilot. The numbers in brackets refer to items in the Royal Air Force loss list in Appendix G.

Unit	Aircraft	Pilot, Fate of Crew	Remarks
Lehr Geschwader 1			
1. V Gruppe	Me 110 3802 destroyed	Oblt Mueller 2 killed	Shot down by Sgt O'Manney 229 Sqn. Crashed near Ashford at 3.15 p.m.
2. V Gruppe	Me 110 destroyed	Lt Gorisch 2 killed	Failed to return from sortie over England. Crashed into sea.
3. V Gruppe	Me 110 destroyed	Lt Adametz 2 missing	Failed to return from sortie over England. Believed crashed into sea.
Lehr Geschwader 2			
4. I Gruppe	Me 109 2061 destroyed	Uffz Streibing captured	Shot down by fighter. Pilot bailed out. Crashed near Rainham at about 3 p.m.
5. I Gruppe	Me 109 2058 destroyed	Uffz Klik captured	Believed shot down by Fg Off Haines 19 Sqn. Crash-landed at Shellness at 2.45 p.m.
Fighter Geschwader 3			
6. Stab	Me 109 5205 destroyed	Oberstlt von Wedel captured	Shot down by fighter. Pilot attempted a forced landing at Bilsington at about 12 p.m. Aircraft struck farm building killing two civilians.

Unit	Aircraft	Pilot, Fate of Crew	Remarks
7. I Gruppe	Me 109 0945 destroyed	Fw Vollner killed	Dived into English Channel at about 12.30 p.m., returning from a combat sortie over England. Reason not apparent to German pilots flying nearby.
8. I Gruppe	Me 109 1563 destroyed	Ofw Buchholz wounded	Aircraft damaged in combat with fighters. Ditched in English Channel at about 3.30 p.m. Pilot picked up by German rescue service.
9. I Gruppe	Me 109 2685 destroyed	Ofw Hessel captured	Shot down by fighter. Pilot bailed out. Crashed near Tenterden at about 2.45 p.m.
10. I Gruppe	Me 109 1606 destroyed	Oblt Reum- schuessel captured	Probably shot down by Sgt Bailey, 603 Sqn. Pilot bailed out. Crashed near Charing at 2.45 p.m.

Fighter Geschwader 27

Unit	Aircraft	Pilot, Fate of Crew	Remarks
11. I Gruppe	Me 109 6249 damaged	Pilot unhurt	Ran out of fuel on return from sortie over England. Forced-landed in northern France.
12. I Gruppe	Me 109 6232 destroyed	Oblt Ahrens missing	Missing after a sortie over England. Probably crashed in sea.
13. I Gruppe	Me 109 6147 destroyed	Uffz Walburger captured	Possibly shot down by Sgt Cox 19 Sqn. Forced-landed near Uckfield at about 12.30 p.m.
14. I Gruppe	Me 109 3875 destroyed	Gefr Elles wounded	Crashed on landing at base with battle damage on return from sortie over England.

Fighter Geschwader 51

Unit	Aircraft	Pilot, Fate of Crew	Remarks
15. III Gruppe	Me 109 3266 destroyed	Lt Bildau captured	Shot down by fighter. Pilot bailed out. Crashed near Dover at 2.45 p.m.

Unit		Aircraft	Pilot, Fate of Crew	Remarks
16.	III Gruppe	Me 109 2803 destroyed	Fw Klotz killed	Shot down by fighter. Crashed near Brenchley at 2.30 p.m.

Fighter Geschwader 52

17.	I Gruppe	Me 109 3182 destroyed	Lt Bethel captured	Collided with Hurricane (No. 20). Pilot bailed out. Crashed near Staplehurst at 11.50 a.m.

Fighter Geschwader 53

18.	I Gruppe	Me 109 6160 destroyed	Uffz Schersand killed	Failed to return from sortie over England.
19.	I Gruppe	Me 109 5197 destroyed	Fw Tschoppe captured	Shot down by fighter. Pilot bailed out. Crashed near Canterbury at about noon.
20.	I Gruppe	Me 109 destroyed	Oblt Schmidt killed	Shot down by Plt Off Macphail of 603 Sqn. Pilot bailed out but parachute failed to open. Crashed on Bearsted golf course at about 12.20 p.m.
21.	I Gruppe	Me 109 5111 damaged	Pilot unhurt	Forced-landed with battle damage at Etaples after combat sortie over England.
22.	I Gruppe	Me 109 1590 destroyed	Oblt Haase killed	Shot down by Fg Off Nesbitt of 1 RCAF Sqn. Pilot bailed out but parachute failed to open. Crashed near Biggin Hill at about noon.
23.	I Gruppe	Me 109 3619 destroyed	Uffz Feldmann captured	Shot down by fighter. Crash-landed near Dymchurch at about 12.40 p.m.
24.	I Gruppe	Me 109 1345 destroyed	Ofw Mueller captured	Probably crashed into sea.
25.	III Gruppe	Me 109 5251 destroyed	Pilot unhurt	Ditched in Channel after sortie over England. Pilot picked up by German rescue service.

Unit		Aircraft	Pilot, Fate of Crew	Remarks
26.	III Gruppe	Me 109 1174 destroyed	Pilot unhurt	Crashed and burnt out at Etaples after sortie over England.

Fighter Geschwader 77

27.	I Gruppe	Me 109 3759 destroyed	Oblt Kunze killed	Shot down by F Sgt Unwin of 19 Sqn. Crashed near Lympne at about 2.50 p.m.
28.	I Gruppe	Me 109 4802 destroyed	Uff Meixner killed	Probably shot down by Plt Off Mather 66 Sqn. Crashed into sea off Dungeness at about 2.55 p.m.
29.	I Gruppe	Me 109 4847 damaged	Pilot unhurt	Forced-landed in northern France with battle damage after sortie over England.

Bomber Geschwader 1

30.	I Gruppe	He 111 damaged beyond repair	3 crew wounded	Attacked by Flt Gillies, Plt Off Mather and Sgt Hunt of 66 Squadron at 7.20 p.m. Crash-landed near St Valery-sur-Somme.

Bomber Geschwader 2

31.	Stab	Dornier 17 damaged	2 crew wounded	Returned with battle damage after sortie over England.
32.	II Gruppe	Dornier 17 2678 destroyed	Oblt Latz 3 captured 1 missing	Shot down by fighters. Crash-landed near Hastings at about 3.15 p.m.
33.	II Gruppe	Dornier 17 2304 destroyed	Uffz Boehme 2 killed 2 missing	Shot down by AA fire, and fighters. Crashed into sea off Dungeness at about 3.20 p.m.
34.	II Gruppe	Dornier 17 1135 damaged	Lt Rohr 1 wounded	Returned with battle damage after sortie over England.
35.	III Gruppe	Dornier 17 2539 damaged	Oblt Schweitring 1 killed	Returned with battle damage after sortie over England.
36.	III Gruppe	Dornier 17 1153 damaged	1 wounded	Returned with battle damage after sortie over England.

Unit	Aircraft	Pilot, Fate of Crew	Remarks
37. III Gruppe	Dornier 17 3401 destroyed	1 killed 1 missing	Shot down by Plt Off Lock 41 Sqn and Plt Off Neil 249 Sqn. Crashed into sea off Clacton at about 3.30 p.m. Two crew picked up by German rescue service.
38. III Gruppe	Dornier 17 2549 destroyed	1 killed 3 missing	Crashed into sea after sortie over England.
39. III Gruppe	Dornier 17 4245 destroyed	1 killed 2 wounded 1 missing	Crashed into sea after sortie over England. Two crew picked up by German rescue service.
40. III Gruppe	Dornier 17 3432 damaged	Hptm Kalepky 1 wounded	Returned to base with battle damage.
41. III Gruppe	Dornier 17 3440 destroyed	Uffz Stampfer 4 captured	Engine shot out by Sgt Garton 73 Sqn. Finished off by AA fire from Chatham defences. Crew bailed out. Crashed at Chatham at 3.05 p.m.
42. III Gruppe	Dornier 17 3405 destroyed	Fw Staib 2 killed 2 captured	Shot down by Plt Off Patullo 46 Sqn. Crashed into sea off Herne Bay at about 3.20 p.m. Two crew rescued by Royal Navy.
43. III Gruppe	Dornier 17 3230 destroyed	Uffz Krummheuer 3 killed 1 captured	Shot down by fighters. Crashed near Cranbrook at about 2.45 p.m.

Bomber Geschwader 3

Unit	Aircraft	Pilot, Fate of Crew	Remarks
44. II Gruppe	Dornier 17 2879 damaged	Lt Schopper 2 wounded	Returned to base with battle damage.
45. II Gruppe	Dornier 17 3457 destroyed	Lt Michaelis 3 killed 1 captured	Damaged by AA fire, finished off by Sqn Ldr Sample 504 Sqn. Crashed near Dartford at 2.45 p.m.
46. II Gruppe	Dornier 17 2881 destroyed	Fw von Goertz 4 captured	Shot down by Plt F Sgt Steere 19 and Plt Off Fejfar 310 Sqn. Crash-landed on Isle of Grain at 2.45 p.m.

Unit		Aircraft	Pilot, Fate of Crew	Remarks
47.	II Gruppe	Dornier 17 3294 destroyed	Lt Duemler 3 killed 1 captured	Shot down by Fg Off Hardacre 504 Sqn and Plt Off Barclay 249 Sqn. Crashed near Billericay at 2.33 p.m.
48.	II Gruppe	Dornier 17 1176 destroyed	Oblt Langenhein 1 killed 2 missing 1 captured	Probably shot down by Fg Off Neil 249 Sqn. Crashed into Thames Estuary.
49.	II Gruppe	Dornier 17 3458 destroyed	4 missing	Rammed by Hurricane (No. 60). Crashed near Goudhurst at 2.25 p.m.
50.	II Gruppe	Dornier 17 2649 damaged	1 wounded	Returned to base with battle damage.
51.	II Gruppe	Dornier 17 4200 destroyed	Ofw Rilling 1 killed 3 captured	Rammed by Hurricane (No. 59). Crashed near Marden at 2.30 p.m.
52.	II Gruppe	Dornier 17 3470 damaged	1 killed	Returned to base with battle damage.
53.	II Gruppe	Dornier 17 4237 damaged	Fw Schultz 1 wounded	Returned to base with battle damage.

Bomber Geschwader 4

54.	II Gruppe	He 111 3086 damaged	Crew unhurt	Returned to base with battle damage, probably from AA fire, after a night sortie over London during the morning darkness.

Bomber Geschwader 26

55.	I Gruppe	He 111 6985 destroyed	5 captured	Shot down after being attacked by several fighters. Sqn Ldr McNab of 1 RCAF, Plt Off Baker of 41, Plt Offs Cochrane and Mortimer of 257, and Sgts Prchal and Rechka of 310 Sqn. Crash-landed at Asplens Head, Foulness, at about 3.15 p.m.

Unit	Aircraft	Pilot, Fate of Crew	Remarks
56. I Gruppe	He 111 5609 damaged	Crew unhurt	Returned to base with battle damage.
57. I Gruppe	He 111 5612 damaged	Lt Cescotti Crew unhurt	Returned to base with damage after attack by Plt Off Pease of 603i Sqn.
58. II Gruppe	He 111 6849 damaged	2 wounded	Crash-landed at base with battle damage.

Bomber Geschwader 53

Unit	Aircraft	Pilot, Fate of Crew	Remarks
59. Stab	He 111 3140 destroyed	Fw Schweiger 4 killed 1 missing	Shot down after being attacked by several fighters. Crashed beside Woolwich Arsenal at about 3 p.m.
60. I Gruppe	He 111 5120 destroyed	Lt Boeckh 1 killed 4 captured	Shot down by fighters. Crashed near Grays at 2.55 p.m.
61. I Gruppe	He 111 5481 destroyed	Uffz Lehner 2 killed 3 captured	Shot down by fighters. Crashed near Sandhurst at about 3.25 p.m.
62. I Gruppe	He 111 5494 damaged	3 wounded	Forced-landed near Boulogne with battle damage.
63. II Gruppe	He 111 6843 destroyed	Ofw Schmidt-born 1 killed 4 captured	Forced out of formation by hit from AA fire. Attacked by several fighters and shot down. Crash-landed near Staplehurst at about 3.25 p.m.
64. II Gruppe	He 111 5718 destroyed	Lt Baensch 2 killed 3 captured	Shot down by several fighters, including Sgts Lacey of 501 and Parsons of 504 Sqns. Crashed near Benenden at about 2.50 p.m.
65. II Gruppe	He 111 2771 destroyed	Fw Behrendt 2 killed 3 captured	Shot down by several fighters, including Fg Off Lochnan of 1 RCAF, Sgts Hunt and Parsons of 66, Plt Offs Hill and Mottram of 92, Flt Lt Rimmer and Plt Offs Bright and

Unit	Aircraft	Pilot, Fate of Crew	Remarks
			Simpson of 229, Plt Off Stansfield of 242 and Sqn Ldr Sample of 504 Sqn. Crash-landed on West Malling airfield at about 3 p.m.
66. II Gruppe	He 111 damaged	1 killed	Returned to base with battle damage after sortie over England.
67. III Gruppe	He 111 damaged	2 wounded	Returned to base with battle damage after sortie over England.
68. III Gruppe	He 111 3340 damaged	2 wounded	Forced-landed near Armentières with battle damage.
Bomber Geschwader 55			
69. III Gruppe	He 111 1586 destroyed	3 killed	Shot down by Spitfires of 152 Sqn. Crashed into sea off Portland. Two crew picked up by German rescue service.
70. III Gruppe	He 111 2815 damaged	Ofw Brauckmann 1 killed 1 wounded	Returned to base with battle damage.
Bomber Geschwader 76			
71. I Gruppe	Dornier 17 2361 destroyed	Oblt Zehbe 3 killed 2 captured	Attacked by several fighters over London, including Plt Off Cochrane of 257, Plt Off Chalupa of 302, Flt Lt Jeffries and Sgts Hubacek, Kaucky and Puda of 310, Sqn Ldr Sample of 504, Fg Off Ogilvie of 609 Sqn. Then Sgt Holmes of 504 Sqn (No. 50) rammed it. Crashed beside Victoria stn at 12.10 p.m.
72. I Gruppe	Dornier 17 2651 destroyed	Ofw Niebler 3 killed 2 captured	Shot down by several fighters, including Flt Lts Gillies and Leather and Plt Offs Bodie of 66 and

Unit	Aircraft	Pilot, Fate of Crew	Remarks
			Pollard of 611, Plt Off Meaker of 249 Sqn. Crashed near Sturry at 12.40 p.m.
73. I Gruppe	Dornier 17 2364 damaged beyond repair	Oblt Hermann 1 killed 2 wounded	Crash-landed near Boulogne with battle damage.
74. I Gruppe	Dornier 17 2524 damaged beyond repair	Uffz Figge 1 wounded	Forced-landed near Poix with battle damage.
75. I Gruppe	Dornier 17 damaged	Uffz Hanke Crew unhurt	Returned with battle damage.
76. I Gruppe	Dornier 17 damaged	Fw Uhlmann 1 wounded	Returned with battle damage.
77. III Gruppe	Dornier 17 2578 destroyed	Fw Keck 2 killed 2 missing	Forced out of formation during attacks by fighters over London. Finished off by Plt Off Barton 253 Sqn. Crashed into sea off Herne Bay at about 12.30 p.m.
78. III Gruppe	Dornier 17 2555 destroyed	Fw Heitsch 1 killed 3 captured	Damaged initially by Sgt Holmes, 504 Sqn. Finished off by Plt Off Lawson 19, Plt Off Crossman 46, Plt Off Mortimer 257 Sqns. Crash-landed near Sevenoaks at about 12.20 p.m.
79. III Gruppe	Dornier 17 2814 destroyed	Lt Wagner 4 killed	Attacked initially by F Sgt Kominek of 310 Sqn. Finished off by Sgts Hurry and Jeffries of 46, Plt Off Ortmans and Sgt O'Manney of 229 and Plt Off White of 504 Sqn. Crashed near Uckfield at about 12.30 p.m.

Unit	Aircraft	Pilot, Fate of Crew	Remarks
80. III Gruppe	Dornier 17 3322 destroyed	Fw Raab 1 killed 3 captured	Forced to leave formation after suffering battle damage. Finished off by Sqn Ldr Lane of 19, Sgt Tyrer of 46, Flt Lt Villa of 72, Plt Off Turner of 242, Flt Brothers and Plt Off Mortimer of 257, Sgt Wright of 605 Sqn. Crashed near Sevenoaks at about 12.20 p.m.

Note: there is evidence that other Dorniers of Bomber Geschwader 76 suffered lesser amounts of battle damage during the action but were not listed in the unit's loss return.

Weather Reconnaissance Staffel 51

81.	He 111 6938 destroyed	5 missing	Shot down by Fg Off David and Plt Off Jay of 87 Sqn. Crashed into sea off Salcombe at about 8.45 a.m.

Air Sea Rescue Flight 3

82.	Heinkel 59 floatplane 1513 destroyed	Crew unhurt	Crashed when alighting on sea during rescue mission off Dieppe. Crew rescued.

Coastal Patrol Gruppe 406

83. 3 Staffel	Dornier 18 flying boat 0810 destroyed	Crew unhurt	Crashed taking off from open sea, south of Ireland. Crew rescued.

Appendix G

ROYAL AIR FORCE FIGHTER COMMAND LOSSES, 15 SEPTEMBER 1940

In this section a 'combat loss' is any aircraft destroyed or damaged while engaged in a combat mission, whatever the cause. The numbers in brackets refer to items in the Luftwaffe loss list in Appendix F.

Unit	Aircraft	Pilot, Fate of Crew	Remarks
No. 1 (RCAF) Squadron			
1.	Hurricane P3080 destroyed	Fg Off Nesbitt wounded	Shot down in action with Me 109, believed by Uffz Quezla of I/FG 53. Pilot bailed out. Crashed near Tunbridge Wells at 12.10 p.m.
2.	Hurricane P3876 destroyed	Fg Off Smither killed	Shot down in action with Me 109s. Crashed near Staplehurst at about 12.10 p.m.
3.	Hurricane L1973 damaged	Fg Off Yuile wounded	Returned with battle damage after action with Me 109s and He 111s at about 2.45 p.m.
No. 19 Squadron			
4.	Spitfire R6991	S/Lt Blake unhurt	Forced-landed with battle damage at about 3 p.m.
5.	Spitfire X4070 destroyed	Sgt Potter prisoner	Shot down over English Channel at about 3 p.m. Pilot picked up by German rescue service.
6.	Spitfire P9431 damaged	Sgt Roden wounded	Crash-landed with battle damage at about 3.10 p.m.
No. 25 Squadron			
7.	Beaufighter R2067 destroyed	Fg Off Miley 3 killed	Circumstances of this loss unclear. Crashed near Biggin Hill at 6.20 p.m. On this day Fw Neuhoff of FG 53 claimed to have destroyed a 'Blenheim', but none was lost and the claim may refer to this aircraft.

Appendices

Unit	Aircraft	Pilot, Fate of Crew	Remarks
No. 41 Squadron			
8.	Spitfire P9324 destroyed	Plt Off Langley killed	Shot down in combat with Me 109s at 12.30 p.m. Crashed near Thurrock.
No. 46 Squadron			
9.	Hurricane N2599 damaged	Sgt Hurry unhurt	Returned with damage following combat near London at 12.30 p.m.
10.	Hurricane N2497 damaged	Plt Off Patullo unhurt	Overshot the runway at Stapleford Tawney on return from a combat mission at 3.15 p.m.
No. 66 Squadron			
11.	Spitfire damaged	Plt Off Bodie unhurt	Damaged by return fire from German bombers.
12.	Spitfire damaged	Pilot unhurt	Damaged, probably by return fire from German bombers.
No. 73 Squadron			
13.	Hurricane P3865 destroyed	Plt Off Marchand killed	Shot down in combat with Me 109. Crashed near Faversham at 12.12 p.m.
No. 92 Squadron			
14.	Spitfire R6767 damaged	Sg Sydney unhurt	Returned with battle damage.
15.	Spitfire P9513 damaged.	Plt Off Bartley unhurt	Hit by return fire from Do 17s at about 3 p.m.
16.	Spitfire R6606 destroyed	Plt Off R. Holland wounded	Shot down at 2.50 p.m., probably by Hptm Losigkeit of FG 26. Pilot bailed out. Crashed near Ashford at 2.50 p.m.
No. 213 Squadron			
17.	Hurricane P3113 destroyed	Sgt Llewellyn wounded	Shot down in action by Me 110s. Pilot bailed out. Crashed near Tenterden at about 3 p.m.
18.	Hurricane destroyed	Sgt Croskell unhurt	Shot down during mid-afternoon action. Pilot bailed out. Crashed near Maidstone.

165

Unit	Aircraft	Pilot, Fate of Crew	Remarks
19.	Hurricane damaged	Pilot unhurt	Crash-landed at Detling after combat sortie.

No. 229 Squadron

Unit	Aircraft	Pilot, Fate of Crew	Remarks
20.	Hurricane N2537 destroyed	Plt Off Doutrepont killed	Collided with Me 109, (No. 17). Crashed on Staplehurst station at 11.50 a.m.
21.	Hurricane V6616 destroyed	Plt Off R. Smith wounded	Shot down in engagement with Do 17s. Pilot bailed out. Crashed near Staplehurst at about noon.

No. 238 Squadron

Unit	Aircraft	Pilot, Fate of Crew	Remarks
22.	Hurricane L2089 damaged	Plt Off Simmonds unhurt	Returned to base with battle damage following mid-afternoon action.
23.	Hurricane P2836 destroyed	Sgt Pidd killed	Shot down during mid-afternoon action. Crashed at Pembury.
24.	Hurricane P3920 damaged	Flt Lt Blake unhurt	Damaged in action with He 111s at 3.05 p.m. Forced-landed at West Malling airfield.
25.	Hurricane P3462 damaged	Fg Off Davis unhurt	Returned to base with damage after mid-afternoon action.
26.	Hurricane P3833 damaged	Plt Off Covington unhurt	Damaged in action with He 111s during mid-afternoon action. Forced-landed near East Grinstead.

No. 242 Squadron

Unit	Aircraft	Pilot, Fate of Crew	Remarks
27.	Hurricane V6576 damaged	Flt Lt Ball unhurt	Forced-landed with battle damage after noon action.
28.	Hurricane P2884 destroyed	Flt Lt Powell-Sheddon wounded	Shot down by Me 109. Pilot bailed out. Crashed near Rye at 2.40 p.m.
29.	Hurricane P3515 damaged	Sub Lt Cork unhurt	Damaged in combat with Me 109s during mid-afternoon action. Landed at Rochford airfield.

No. 249 Squadron

Unit	Aircraft	Pilot, Fate of Crew	Remarks
30.	Hurricane damaged beyond repair	Plt Off Lofts unhurt	Severely damaged during mid-afternoon, suffered further damage in crash landing at West Malling airfield.

Unit	Aircraft	Pilot, Fate of Crew	Remarks
No. 253 Squadron			
31.	Hurricane V6698 damaged	Plt Off Barton unhurt	Damaged by return fire from bombers during mid-afternoon action. Forced-landed at Hawkinge airfield.
No. 257 Squadron			
32.	Hurricane P3642 damaged	Plt Off Capon unhurt	Damaged during noon action. Forced-landed at Croydon airfield.
33.	Hurricane damaged	Flt Lt Brothers unhurt	Damaged by return fire from Do 17s during noon action. Forced-landed at Biggin Hill airfield.
No. 302 Squadron			
34.	Hurricane P2954 destroyed	Flt Lt Chlopik killed	Shot down during mid-afternoon action. Crashed near Battlesbridge at 2.45 p.m.
35.	Hurricane destroyed	Plt Off Lapka wounded	Shot down during mid-afternoon action by return fire from Do 17s. Pilot bailed out. Crashed near Pitsea.
36.	Hurricane P3935 damaged	Sgt Kowalski unhurt	Returned to base with battle damage after mid-afternoon action.
37.	Hurricane damaged	Plt Off Kaiwowski unhurt	Forced-landed in field after gun door came open in flight during mid-afternoon action.
No. 303 Squadron			
38.	Hurricane P2903 damaged	Plt Off Lokuciewski wounded	Returned to base with battle damage following noon action.
39.	Hurricane P3939	Sgt Andruszkov unhurt	Shot down in action with Me 109 during mid-afternoon action, believed by Uffz Koppenschlaeger of FG 53. Pilot bailed out. Crashed near Stoke, Isle of Grain.
40.	Hurricane V7465 damaged	Sqn Ldr Kellet unhurt	Damaged in combat with Me 109s during mid-afternoon action.
41.	Hurricane L2099 damaged	Fg Off Zak unhurt	Damaged in combat with Me 109s during mid-afternoon action.

Unit	Aircraft	Pilot, Fate of Crew	Remarks
42.	Hurricane V6673 damaged	Sgt Wojciechowski unhurt	Damaged in combat with Me 109s during mid-afternoon action.
43.	Hurricane R2685 damaged	Plt Off Feric unhurt	Damaged in combat with Me 109s.
44.	Hurricane V6684 damaged	Fg Off Urbanowicz unhurt	Damaged in combat with Me 109s during mid-afternoon action.
45.	Hurricane P3577 destroyed	Sgt Brzezowski missing	Failed to return after mid- afternoon action. Believed to have crashed in Thames Estuary.

No. 310 Squadron

Unit	Aircraft	Pilot, Fate of Crew	Remarks
46.	Hurricane R4087 destroyed	Sgt Hubacek wounded	Shot down by Maj Galland of FG 26. Pilot bailed out. Believed to have crashed on Isle of Grain at about 2.30 p.m.
47.	Hurricane R4085 destroyed	Sqn Ldr Hess unhurt	Shot down by Oblt Horten of FG 26. Pilot bailed out. Crashed near Billericay at about 2.30 p.m.

No. 501 Squadron

Unit	Aircraft	Pilot, Fate of Crew	Remarks
48.	Hurricane V7433 damaged	Sqn Ldr Hogan unhurt	Damaged in combat with Me 109s during noon action. Made wheels-down landing in a field near Sevenoaks.
49.	Hurricane P2760 destroyed	Plt Off Hove d'Ertsenrijck killed	Shot down by Me 109s. Broke up in mid-air. Wreckage fell near Chilham.

No. 504 Squadron

Unit	Aircraft	Pilot, Fate of Crew	Remarks
50.	Hurricane P2725 destroyed	Sgt Holmes wounded	Rammed Do 17 (No. 71) over central London during noon action. Pilot bailed out. Crashed at Chelsea.
51.	Hurricane L1913 damaged	Fg Off Royce unhurt	Damaged in combat during noon action.
52.	Hurricane N2481 destroyed	Plt Off Gurteen killed	Shot down. Crashed near Longfield at 1 p.m.
53.	Hurricane N2705 destroyed	Fg Off Jebb fatally wounded	Shot down in combat during mid-afternoon action. Crashed near Dartford.

Unit	Aircraft	Pilot, Fate of Crew	Remarks
No. 602 Squadron			
54.	Spitfire X4412 damaged	Sgt Babbage unhurt	Damaged by return fire from Do 17s during mid-afternoon action. Forced-landed near Shoreham.
No. 603 Squadron			
55.	Spitfire X4324 destroyed	Plt Off Pease killed	Shot down by an Me 109. Crashed near Kingswood at about 3 p.m.
56.	Spitfire R7019 destroyed	Sqn Ldr Denholm unhurt	Shot down by return fire from Do 17s of BG 3. Pilot bailed out. Crashed near Hastings at 3.10 p.m.
No. 605 Squadron			
57.	Hurricane L2122 destroyed	Plt Off Jones wounded	Shot down in combat with Me 109s near Tonbridge. Pilot bailed out. Crashed near Plaxtol at 11.40 a.m.
58.	Hurricane P3580 damaged	Flt Lt Currant unhurt	Damaged by return fire from Do 17s during noon action.
59.	Hurricane L2012 destroyed	Plt Off Cooper-Slipper wounded	Damaged by return fire from Do 17s of BG 3. Rammed Do 17 (No. 51). Pilot bailed out. Crashed near Marden at about 2.30 p.m.
No. 607 Squadron			
60.	Hurricane V6688 destroyed	Plt Off Stephenson wounded	Rammed Do 17 (No. 49). Pilot bailed out. Crashed near Cranbrook at about 2.25 p.m.
No. 609 Squadron			
61.	Spitfire K9997 damaged	Plt Off Tobin unhurt	Damaged in landing accident on return from noon action.
62.	Spitfire R6690 destroyed	Plt Off Gaunt killed	Shot down during noon action. Dived into ground near Kenley at about 12.30 p.m.
63.	Spitfire R6922 damaged	Fg Off Dundas unhurt	Damaged by return fire from Do 17s during mid-afternoon action.

Unit	Aircraft	Pilot, Fate of Crew	Remarks
No. 611 Squadron			
64.	Spitfire P7303 damaged	Fg Off Williams unhurt	Damaged by return fire from He 111s during mid-afternoon action.

BIBLIOGRAPHY

Books

Balke, Ulf, *Kampfgeschwader 100*, Motorbuch Verlag, Stuttgart, 1981.

Barclay, George, *Angels 22*, Arrow Books, London, 1971.

Barker, E. C., *The Fighter Aces of the R.A.F.*, William Kimber, London, 1964.

Bekker, Cajus, *The Luftwaffe War Diaries*, Macdonald, London, 1964.

Bickers, Richard Townsend, *Ginger Lacey, Fighter Pilot*, Robert Hale, London, 1962.

Bishop, Edward, *Their Finest Hour*, Ballantine, New York, 1968.

Boorman, H. R. P., *Hell's Corner 1940*, Kent Messenger, Maidstone, 1943.

Brickhill, Paul, *Reach for the Sky*, Collins, London, 1957.

Bruetting, Georg, *Das waren die Deutschen Kampflieger Asse 1939–1945*, Motorbuch Verlag, Stuttgart, 1975.

Carne, Daphne, *The Eyes of the Few*, Macmillan, London, 1970.

Churchill, Winston, *The Second World War*, Volume 2, Cassell, London, 1948.

Collier, Basil, *The Defence of the United Kingdom*, HMSO, London, 1952.

Collier, Richard, *Eagle Day*, Hodder and Stoughton London, 1972

Dierich, Wolfgang, *Die Verbaende der Luftwaffe 1935–1945*, Motorbuch Verlag, Stuttgart, 1976.

——, *Kampfgeschwader 55*, Motorbuch Verlag, Stuttgart, 1975.

Elan (pen name of Sqn Ldr Brian Lane), *Spitfire Pilot*, John Murray, London, 1944.

Forrester, Larry, *Fly For Your Life*, Frederick Muller, London, 1962.

Galland, Adolf, *The First and the Last*, Methuen, London, 1955.

Green, William, *Warplanes of the Third Reich*, Macdonald and Jane's, London, 1970.

Grinnell-Milne, Duncan, *The Silent Victory, September 1940*, Bodley Head, London, 1958.

Grundelach, Karl, *Kampfgeschwader 4*, Motorbuch Verlag, Stuttgart, 1978.

Hinsley, F. W., *British Intelligence in the Second World War*, Volume 1, HMSO, London, 1979.

Wartime HMSO Official Publications (authors not named):
  Front Line 1940–41. The Story of Civil Defence
  Roof Over Britain. The story of the AA Defences
  The Battle of Britain
Kiehl, Heinz, *Kampfgeschwader 53*, Motorbuch Verlag, Stuttgart, 1983.
McKee, Alexander, *Strike from the Sky*, Souvenir Press, London, 1960.
Mason, Francis, *Battle over Britain*, McWhirter Twins, London, 1969.
Neil, *Gun Button to Fire*, William Kimber, London, 1987.
Obermaier, Ernst, *Die Ritterkreuztraeger der Luftwaffe, Jagdflieger 1939–45*, Verlag Diether Hoffmann, Mainz, 1966.
Price, Alfred, *Battle of Britain, The Hardest Day*, Arms and Armour Press, London, 1988.
——, *Blitz on Britain*, Ian Allan, Shepperton, 1977.
——, *Luftwaffe Handbook*, Ian Allan, Shepperton, 1986.
——, *Combat Development in World War Two: Fighter Aircraft*, Arms and Armour Press, London, 1989.
——, *The Spitfire Story*, Arms and Armour Press, London, 1986.
——, *Combat Development in World War Two: Bomber Aircraft*, Arms and Armour Press, London, 1989.
Ramsey, Winston, *et al*, *The Battle of Britain, Then And Now*, After the Battle, London, 1980.
Rawlings, John, *Fighter Squadrons of the R.A.F.*, Macdonald and Jane's, London, 1969.
Shore, Christopher, and Williams, Clive, *Aces High*, Neville Spearman, London, 1966.
Woods, Derek, and Dempster, Derek, *The Narrow Margin*, Hutchinson, London, 1961.
Wright, Robert, *Dowding and the Battle of Britain*, Macdonald and Jane's, London, 1972.

Magazine articles
Allward, Maurice, and Hooton, Ted, 'Battle of Britain Day, 15th September 1940', *Air Pictorial*, September 1975.
Macmillan, Wing Commander Norman, 'Resolving the War's Great Controversy', *Aeronautics*, October and November 1960.
Marrs, Eric, '152 Squadron: A Personal Diary of the Battle of Britain', *The Aeroplane*, 14 September 1945.
The War Illustrated, 27 September 1940.

Newspapers
Daily Express, 16 September 1940.
Stratford Express, 20 September 1940.
Sunday Times, 15 September 1940.
Times, 16 September 1940.
Voelkische Beobachter, 15 and 17 September 1940.

Unpublished sources

Air Ministry, '*Air Defence of the United Kingdom*', copy held in the Public Record Office, Kew.

Pilots' combat reports, Fighter Command, Group and station records, Anti-Aircraft Command records, Home Office records, all held in the Public Record Office, Kew.

German records held at the Bundesarchiv Militaerarchiv, Freiburg, Germany.

Luftwaffe Quartermaster's Loss Returns, microfilm held at Imperial War Museum Library, London.

INDEX

A figure 2 in brackets after a page reference means that there are two separate references to the subject on that page. In indexing the Appendices, the following have been omitted: Luftwaffe airfields in Appendix C, and crew members in Appendix F.

175

Index